Leading
Women

Leading Women

How Church Women Can
Avoid Leadership Traps and
Negotiate the Gender Maze

Carol E. Becker

Abingdon Press
Nashville

LEADING WOMEN

Copyright © 1996 by Abingdon Press

This book is printed on recycled, acid-free paper.

Library of Congress Cataloging-in-Publication Data

Becker, Carol E.
    Leading women/Carol E. Becker.
        p.   cm.
    Includes bibliographical references.
    ISBN 0-687-45964-8 (pbk.: alk. paper)
    1. Christian leadership.   2. Women clergy.   3. Women church
officers.   4. Women in Christianity.   5. Feminism—Religious
aspects—Christianity.   I. Title.
    BV652.1.B38   1996
    262′.14′082—dc20   95-41434
                                                                                              CIP

Scripture quotations, unless otherwise indicated, are from the *New Revised Standard Version Bible*,
copyright © 1989, by the Division of Christian Education of the National Council of the
Churches of Christ in the United States of America.

Scripture quotations noted JB are from *The Jerusalem Bible*, copyright © 1966 by Darton,
Longman & Todd, Ltd. and Doubleday & Company, Inc. Used by permission of the publishers.

96 97 98 99 00 01 02 03 04 05 — 10 9 8 7 6 5 4 3 2

MANUFACTURED IN THE UNITED STATES OF AMERICA

To the memory
of
my grandmothers,
Olivia Mix Wiederanders
and
Louise Hast Becker

They served before me.

Wisdom has built her house,
she has hewn her seven pillars.
She has slaughtered her animals,
she has mixed her wine,
she has also set her table.
She has sent out her servant girls, she calls
from the highest places in the town,
"You that are simple, turn in here!"
To those without sense she says,
"Come, eat of my bread
and drink of the wine I have mixed.
Lay aside immaturity, and live,
and walk in the way of insight."

Proverbs 9:1-6

Contents

Acknowledgments

The chorus of voices speaking in this book includes the voices of women and men in leadership throughout the established Protestant denominations. These leaders spoke in interviews and focus groups, and also conducted focus groups to help complete the project. My first thanks must be for them, and for what they have shared with me. Indeed, I cannot thank them enough, for this is really their book. Without reservation, they have been candid and thoughtful. They have shared their own joys and disappointments. They have expressed hope for the future of the church. Though they remain anonymous to all but me, their voices are loud and clear.

I owe particular thanks to others as well. The women of my own denomination who supported me in the writing of this book will never know how much their prayers and their words of encouragement helped. Cynthia Hileman and Rebecca von Fischer, who have answered the call to become clergy in the course of the twenty years I have known them as best of friends, are always a special inspiration to me and a counterpoint to my own decision to serve as a laywoman. Claire Buettner deserves special mention for her gracious assistance in the Evangelical Lutheran Church in America library. Lynn Entine has modeled the life of a writer and thus taught me how to be about this task. Paul Edison-Swift provided emergency technical support when the computers threatened to foil the final draft. Roger Heuser provided research expertise and feedback as well as the essential encouragement of an enlightened male. Add to these the many women thoroughly the denominations who heard about the project and continued to inquire of its progress. Their interest, too, was a boon to my courage to speak. A special thank you also to the men of the church who asked questions, wondered, and understood that this book is necessary also for them.

My colleagues at Growth Design Corporation deserve special mention for their constant support at work every day, and their pride in this project. It is always a challenge to have a colleague writing a book. It means extra work for everyone in the office, and they were always up to the challenge. I am deeply grateful to Byron Tweeten and Wendy Lundquist, who put the full resources of this fine consulting group at my disposal. Thanks, too, to my clients, who were patient with my writing schedule and very encouraging in the last months before deadline. Particular thanks are due to Kay Edwards, Diane Walker, Sue Stelter, and Mary Behrendt who formed my office support team. Books don't get written without researchers, typists, and proofreaders.

Closer still to this project are those who helped make it possible. The book would not have been written without the suggestions, encouragement, mentoring, and direct support of Norman Shawchuck. He also provided the focus group process and connected me to many people who were willing to help run groups. Thus the circles widened so that more and more people provided insights for the future of women and men working together in the church. My editor Paul Franklyn also deserves many thanks. He is truly a man who knows how to be collaborative and supportive and instructive all at the same time, and it was my distinct pleasure and privilege to have him by my side as this book unfolded.

Finally, and without doubt most important of all are those closest to my heart, who have walked the walk with me. Jim Lyons and Frank Carillo have each provided courageous professional advice at key moments in my career as a church leader. Craig Lewis and Albert "Pete" Pero were both friends and spiritual counselors in my awakening. Lucy Klein and Ken James walked with me in my own personal journey during the completion of this manuscript. My parents too were encouraging. A special word of thanks is due to my mother, who often has found it difficult to accompany me in my life's journey. This time, she was with me all the way. My children Emily and Ethan understood without any explanation how important this project was. My best friend Judy Braham has modeled a life of faith for me, and was my prayer partner in this journey. My husband Paul has been with me always, in moments of pain and moments of triumph, a loving and steadying support. My humblest thanks to all.

Introduction

This book is about women and men working together in the church. The emphasis is on women and what happens to them in the church. To a lesser extent, it is also about what happens to men when they try to work with women. This book is not an attempt to inflate the feminine or to trash the masculine. It says, above all, that we women want a two-way street.[1] In whatever ways we discover to lead the church together, women want one set of rules for both women and men in leadership.

How and What the Research Tells Us

The first two sections of this book are devoted to a description of the status quo for women in leadership. I investigated largely by talking to women and men systematically, in lengthy interviews. In all, I interviewed thirty-five women and eight men in thirteen different Protestant denominations. I included in my interviews clergy, lay professionals, and women who work as volunteers in denominations that restrict women to that role.[2] Most of what I heard was about women, their issues, their leadership. In the interviews I wanted to learn more about the present situation for women and men in the church, in relation to the emergence of women in leadership. Unless we know our present, how can we plan effectively for a better future? Thus, my questions focused primarily on women in leadership, whether I was interviewing women or men.

Fourteen themes emerged. They are wide-ranging and sometimes unexpected. All of them are thought-provoking and some are difficult to hear, particularly for men. These fourteen themes are amplified throughout the book with forays into parallel evidence from the current literature on leadership. Part 1 is about the church as a workplace for women. Part 2 describes what happens to women who work for the church, and what happens to men when they work with women.

Part 3 is about change. After the interviews, and largely because so many women and men wanted to talk about this subject, I asked them to meet in focus groups to define "what must happen in order for women and men (working together) in church leadership to have a more effective and mutually satisfying ministry with each other?" Over one hundred church leaders participated in the focus groups, and as a result of their conversations with one another, I can suggest ten change factors.

Women and men from throughout the Protestant denominations assisted me by conducting the focus groups among their colleagues. In all, sixteen different leaders held nineteen focus groups in fifteen different locations throughout the U.S. and in Canada, and throughout the denominations. A total of nine denominations were represented in the focus groups. A defined process ensured that each focus group answered the key question and in a way that the results would be reliable.

The change factors summarize what the focus groups tell us. They are outlined in the final chapter of the book. Since the focus groups dealt specifically with a question about the future for women and men in the church, the responses provide us with a prescription for change. They tell us what women and men in church leadership believe must be done in order to create a more mutual and friendly workplace. It is clear from the focus group feedback that both women and men want better ways of working together. Both recognize the benefit of legitimizing women's leadership in the church.

Together, the use of interviews and focus groups to gather information is based on Belenky's fifth "way of knowing," which leads to constructed knowledge.[3] I engaged women and men in a reflective process so that I could, literally, gather their experiences, reflect on them, listen to my own heart and mind, and correlate what I observed and knew myself with existing literature on the subject of women in church leadership. This process of using the particular, personal, and firsthand experience of individual people, including myself, leads to constructed knowledge that is connected rather than separate. I have moved outside what is given (by books, by other theories) to construct what I know about women in church leadership. The women and men who participated have assisted me.

Strictly from a research perspective, the information gathered here provides reliable anecdotal information. It is qualitative rather than quantitative research. It is not statistically valid, and there are no numbers to prove the validity of any idea. Anecdotally, however, this book reflects the lived experiences of women and men in church leadership.

I took this path upon the challenge of a superior of mine in the Evangelical Lutheran Church in America who, after reading my first published article on this subject,[4] became quite angry. "You had better talk to other women before you say these things," he admonished. "I'm sure there are women out there who won't agree with you." I didn't find any.

Interviews and Focus Groups: Different Tones

The interviews and focus groups were different for a number of reasons that are worth noting here. First, they were different processes. Each interview was a one-on-one conversation between the author and a subject. They were confidential in that specific information from them could not be used without masking the identity of the speaker and the specific situations under discussion. The focus groups, on the other hand, were group processes that everyone knew would provide reportable information.

Second, each probe asked a different question. As we have noted previously, the interviews sought information about the status quo. Women and men were asked to be descriptive and to share information about their current or past situations to the extent that they were willing. The focus groups, on the other hand, asked about the future. Specifically, the groups were asked to indicate what must be done to create a better situation for women and men working together.

The answers, predictably, were different. I perceived a different level of feeling and a different tone from each of the two processes. The interviews were engaging, intense, personal, and sometimes critical. Women and men were very candid. For the women particularly, honesty sometimes required negativity. The women were not trying to be negative as if that were a personality trait. They were simply telling their stories as they know them. Some of their stories do not have happy endings. Still, the women stressed, they were speaking candidly so that all the church might know how much positive change is needed.

In the focus groups, on the other hand, there was positive energy. Many participants expressed thanks for the opportunity to participate. One focus group leader wrote, "The most significant time was the discussion. The energy level was high, and many thanked me afterward for the opportunity. More opportunities should be made for such discussion in safe places." Apparently for participants, the focus group provided one such safe place. The overall message: in spite of the negatives, in spite of the discouragements, many women and men in the church still believe that a more universally welcoming environment is possible and worth striving for. I hope so.

A Word to Men Reading This Book

Much in this book will challenge men. The first is its title. A colleague and friend of mine said, upon reading portions of the first draft: "Men will never read this book. This book is about women! Men don't have any reason to read a book about women."

His concern is legitimate, but I don't agree with him. I have too much faith in the integrity of men. Still, I worried about his prediction while I wrote chapters 9 and 10. What my respected friend said illustrates one of the central points of the book. If you read on, you will find out how and why, and you will also learn something about yourself and the women who work with you.

Much is said in this book that will challenge you. Sometimes the assertive way in which I have held men and the patriarchy of the church accountable for the present status of the denominations may even anger you. I would offer you two insights. First, women have been maligned in ways equally as painful and personally damaging at least since the fourth century. (Read chapter 5.) Second, we women must engage in clear separation from men in order to know ourselves. We must define our positions as church leaders. We must establish our territory and mark our boundaries relative to men and to the prevailing paradigm. It's necessary to knowing ourselves and our position in the church workplace. Insofar as this book addresses that task, it is unrelenting and direct. I know—women aren't supposed to be that way, but we have to be sometimes. (Read part 2.)

In case you have any remaining doubts, here are some reasons to read this book:

1. It will help you understand your female peers and the issues they face.
2. It will help you understand yourself better as you learn to work with women.
3. It will save you from making a lot of mistakes.
4. Men always say they want to know what makes women "the way they are." This book will help.
5. You'll know why your own individual support is not enough to improve the workplace for women.
6. It will shed light on how stereotypes and traps hurt both women and men in the church.
7. It could save you from being labeled a "jerk."
8. This book will help if you aren't getting along with your female colleague and you can't figure out why.
9. Men have some interesting things to say in this book.
10. A woman gave it to you and asked you to read it.
11. Some of your friends and colleagues were interviewed for this book.
12. You have courage.
13. You want women in church leadership.
14. You want women to *survive* in church leadership.

The News Keeps On Coming

As this book goes to press, information continues to appear on my desk to verify that it is needed.

First, this headline jumped out at me from my copy of *The Lutheran:* "Vatican Says 'No' to Inclusive Language." It has ruled the NRSV Bible "off limits" for Catholics. The new translation, approved in 1991 by the U.S. Catholic bishops for use in worship, uses "generally inclusive language for terms such as 'man' and 'brother' when it wouldn't alter the meaning of the texts." It retains masculine references to God. Meanwhile, the U.S. Catholic bishops, at their meeting in

November 1994, "declared their belief in the equality of women and men . . . urging more top jobs for women and more inclusive language in religious materials. But they refused to challenge Pope John Paul II's declaration that women can't be priests."[5]

Perhaps, as one clergywoman points out, I should be glad for bishops who have "declared sexism a sin and have affirmed the priesthood of all males."[6] Perhaps I should be glad that they at least tried to institutionalize inclusive language. But I am not. I get angry. I feel sad and discouraged. It's another message to women like too many we have heard before. So I write from my heart, trying to share the passion and love for church that I and so many other women have. I hear behind me a chorus of others who have spoken to me from their hearts.

Then I hear that the head of a major Protestant denomination has taken personal action to bar a woman from a teaching position in theology, a position for which the woman in question is well qualified and was actually the choice of the search committee. While I am simmering over this news, a local clergywoman calls to say that she's been released from presiding at a wedding because the grandfather who is paying the bills "just found out that the clergyman is really a clergywoman, and he doesn't think women should be pastors." So with a thank-you-very-much to this clergywoman, the family has decided to find another church in which to hold their ceremony. And finally, I hear from one of the professional laywomen interviewed for this book. She says that she has just attended her first clergy cluster gathering. She was greeted with the welcome, "I didn't know they allowed wives to come along to these meetings."

There is indeed a chorus of women and men. With my thanks to them, I commend their stories to you.

Part One

Leadership, Women, and the Church

Leadership Embodied

As I reflect on my own life, three experiences stand out to define leadership. The first was during the early 1970s when I became active in a Lutheran congregation on the fringes of a changing neighborhood in my hometown. It was an integrated congregation where pastors and lay people, Caucasian and African American, shared leadership. Together, we struggled mightily to provide meaningful worship and education to both middle class and poor people. One of our innovations was Family Sunday School. We threw out the traditional age-defined classrooms and put everyone together in the parish hall to learn about the faith. Then, because no resources were available to us, we had to write our own. During those first years, we spent long hours writing curricula for mixed age groups so that young could learn from old, white could learn from African American, and so on.

We had many arguments about what to do with Family Sunday School. We worked hard. We studied the Bible. We asked questions about what it might mean to poor children and unemployed adults. These questions caused us to ask more questions about what the Bible meant to those of us who were middle class and white. There were in our Family Sunday School teaching group lay people and clergy, seminary professors, students, and two women, my best friends, who would later become clergy themselves.[1] Somehow in this mix, the distinctions between clergy and lay dissolved. We were simply people of God, working together to pass our faith on to another generation. We never wondered who were the leaders in our group, and who were the followers. We knew somehow that we were all responsible for teaching the faith.

The resources we created were useful. We might have published them, but we never bothered. Years later, we heard about intergenerational learning, we saw it applied to Sunday schools in a variety of curricula, and were both pleased and amused. For us, the creation of Family Sunday School was a desperate effort to save our fledgling education program.

I know now that we were like the early church, where issues of hierarchy and distinctions between lay and clergy, men and women, were subsumed under the need to survive and grow. We were all Lutheran, but our task was to make an often intellectual theology meaningful to the people in the highways and byways of our city. We struggled mightily, studied hard, questioned much, listened intently, and taught weekly to a growing rabble of people of all backgrounds and faiths.

This was leadership. We were like Paul and Peter, arguing whether the gospel was for the Gentiles or for the Jews only. We were like Priscilla and Aquila, Junia, Barnabas, Jael, and Phoebe, all of whom led the early church from its fragile beginnings to a stronger future.

Five years later my son was born, the second of my children to be born prematurely. I was determined this time, as I had been four years earlier with my daughter, to breast-feed him. It was difficult and I returned to a method I had worked out for myself of teaching the premature infant to welcome the breast instead of the bottle. I was successful thanks to determination and the application of advice given by Dr. Benjamin Spock in his 1948 edition of *Baby and Child Care*, in which he described how to care for the premature infant when medical advice is far away or unavailable. Because I was experiencing firsthand the rewards of breast-feeding my child, I knew how much it would mean to other mothers of premature or hard-to-nurse infants.

I wanted to share what I had learned, and so I joined a local group of women who called themselves *doulas*. We were nursing coaches in a time when breast-feeding was just coming out of ill repute as a "trashy" thing for women to do, especially in public. My specialty was helping the moms whose babies were rejecting the breast or who were premature. Over the course of several years, I counseled many mothers in person, on the phone, in the hospital. I advocated with doctors for the role of our work—with limited success. And I wrote about the techniques I had devised. During all of that time, I never thought about myself as a leader. I had no official position, no particular credentials other than my own experience, and certainly no pay. I had only the authority of my own conviction and experience. And I had, of course, the knowledge that other women would benefit from what I had to offer.

We women knew ourselves to be servants. Others in the group had other roles or specialties in counseling moms. We worked together. We were servants to the blessed women who had just given birth. We were Christian, Jewish, Buddhist, agnostic. We were servants. And we all knew that the name we took—*doula*—came from Paul of the Christian Bible. It was he who told us in our name that we were servants.

I see now that we were leaders in the biblical way. Though our work among emerging families had nothing in particular to do with the church, it had something very particular to do with faith formation. We were, after all, helping women develop the human bond with their children that is so essential to faith formation later in life. Perhaps more important, we were humbling ourselves to show the way. We acted like slaves, available always to new mothers and to doctors who would use us. Through each individual situation, and in the lived experiences of countless women, we showed the way back to natural feeding. And today, in that small town, in the wider medical community, and in both the medical and the popular press, no one questions the rightness of what we said and did at that time and in that place.

This too was leadership. Like Sarah and her husband Abraham of the Old Testament, we women were placed in a leadership position and expected to act as God's servants. We followed in the tradition of Ruth and Naomi, of Esther, of Miriam and Moses, of Joseph. We were examples of Paul's diaconal (service to others) gifts.

More recently, when I strayed into a role in the church that everyone recognized publicly as a leadership position, the poor women of Central America reminded me just what true leadership is. I was on a trip with the bishop of my church, working as his official press person on a tour of El Salvador during the civil war in that country. On one particularly hallowed day, we went by jeep into the war zone to visit a repatriated village. The people who lived there had come back to the remains of their town only ten days before we arrived. Most of them lived in tents, in bombed-out buildings, or under rude canvas shelters. As we drove into the town, I could see that the mud was at least ankle deep. Then it started to rain, steadily and hard. In an effort to spare my new and expensive walking shoes, I took them off and followed the bishop around town barefoot. Many women came up to me, spoke something in Spanish that I could not understand, and went on. I wondered why, ashamed of myself that I could not speak their language. When our tour was finished, we returned to the shelter of a small house where we were to receive refreshments—a thick corn gruel—from a very thankful group of the town's leaders. As I came up the walk to the house, a woman ran out to greet me with a bowl of water and a towel. To my shock and surprise, she knelt before me and washed and dried my muddy feet. I was dumbfounded. What was going on here? Later, on the way back to San Salvador, our guide told me that the women had been moved by my gesture of solidarity with them—walking barefoot with them through their town!

I have pondered that experience for all the years since, knowing that it was a holy moment in my life. I now understand "what was going on." The women of that town were demonstrating leadership to me. Of all the women in that group, I was least the leader. It was they who showed me the way. It was they who lived daily in mud and poverty and despair to rebuild lives for themselves, their children, and the men who might never return home. And when they stooped to wash my feet, they were stooping to show me, once more, the way of leadership.

These women were leaders in the tradition of Mary, who anointed the feet of Jesus. They followed in the footsteps of the woman with a flow of blood, whose faith was so great, and of the centurion, who asked Jesus to heal his daughter. They understood implicitly the relationship between Mary and Martha, who hungered for Jesus' words, and at the same time were servants of the household and of the needs of all around them.

A leader humbles herself to show the way. In so doing, she evokes a following. This is the message of the Gospels and is the standard by which the prophets and the kings of the Old Testament were leaders. It is what I learned in Family Sunday School and in being a *doula* and in having my feet washed in a muddy yard in Central America. It is what we see in the life of Jesus and in the dedication of the apostles, both women and men.

From these experiences in my own life, I know that leadership creates community. It breaks down barriers between people. It communicates, and it creates synergy. At the same time, it engenders respect and builds a following among the people for the leader or leaders who have authority. Leadership also creates something new—something that was not there before. It does so because leaders are not afraid to be creative, to think outside the box, to name something new. At the same time that leadership creates synergy, it also creates controversy, because real leaders are willing to take risks, to be prophetic to the community.

The hardest part of this definition, for me as for most women, is that leadership requires authority. Claiming authority presupposes power, and I am ambivalent about power. Perhaps the examples I have shared here have elements of many different kinds of power and the authority that comes with them.[2] Surely I must also see authority as "strands which are woven through" all of my acts as a leader and as an "ever-present dimension of (my) leadership."[3] The point is that my definition of leadership must stress the paradoxical combination of servanthood and authority.

For us as women, the biggest barrier to integrating this aspect of leadership is that we are prisoners of our culture. We associate leadership with dominance, and slavery with bondage. Leadership so often means "authority over" others; therefore it is difficult to use the word to describe authority in community or partnership.[4] This is true both for the church and for the secular world. We look up to people with authority over others. We consider them leaders by virtue of their power over, by their titles, and often we continue to see them as leaders even when that power is abused. Although we increasingly recognize other forms of leadership, the acquisition of power over others is still central to our typical definition.

This view of leadership is problematic for us as women, and for minority persons, even those of us who have achieved authority over others. In our own lives we have been subject to the oppression of misused authority[5] and are reluctant therefore to embrace authority ourselves. It's simple. We who have been victims of a theology of service that reinforces our personal and social inferiority will not see freedom and empowerment in becoming leaders in the patriarchal way.[6]

The other dialectic is equally problematic. It is very difficult for us to embrace the role of *doula*—slave—in becoming leaders. We women have historically been abused by slavery to men, and in the case of African American women, to literal slavery. So much is this a part of our common past that even for those who have suffered no specific abuse, the memory of abuse is embedded in our unconscious. As healthy women, we are therefore very sensitive about embracing the slavery of true servanthood. Our reluctance is not a sign of our weakness, but a sign of our strength.

To claim my definition of leadership, I—together with other women—must separate authority from dominance, and slavery (that is, the literal service of the master to the subject) from bondage. When we have done this, we can embrace the paradox of leadership that is both authoritative and humbling.

I continue to be enriched by more unexpected insights into the nature of leadership.[7] No matter how many times I experience the dilemmas and traps for women in church leadership, I also continue to be unexpectedly overwhelmed with God's grace. It caught me unaware one Sunday recently when I received communion from my new pastor. Like so many others, she is the first clergywoman to serve my congregation. The very image of her standing there before me offering the Body of Christ was startling and comforting. I could see in her just in that instant much of the maternal love that God has for me, and I was surprised by it. My pastor—she—was there to show me the deep compassion of God. This too is leadership.

Chapter One

What Church Women and Men Say About Leadership

Confused by Wonderland, Alice asked the Cheshire cat: "Will you tell me please, which way I ought to go from here?"

The cat replied, "That depends a good deal on where you want to get to." Alice didn't care where, she said, so long as she got "somewhere."

"Oh you're sure to do that," replied the Cheshire cat with a wide sly smile, "if only you walk long enough."

Women in church leadership want to go somewhere too. But they know where, and they also know that they won't get there if they "just keep walking." It will take much more—a sense of direction, a road-map, some knowledge of the geography, helpful people along the way, a good road, good weather, perhaps even a new and unconventional way of traveling.

Many men realize this need for a calling in the right direction. Women currently work in an alien environment, fighting an uphill battle for jobs, status, and even for the opportunity to be effective leaders. Both men and women are adversely affected. In order to change this reality, women and men together must know their journey, and more about how to make it together.

Women are entering church work in significant numbers. In all established denominations, women are indicating a wish to enter the ordained as well as the lay ministry. Women have much to contribute as leaders, and in many ways they are welcomed, by individual men and by denominational policies. At the same time, women are struggling. They report many problems in working with men and in dealing with the hierarchy of denominations. They face a glass ceiling just as impermeable as in any corporation. In some denominations, women have joined the ranks of church leaders in large numbers and are now leaving in numbers just as large. Men, on the other hand, are welcoming, optimistic, appreciative of women, and also afraid, resentful, confused, and sexist in their treatment of women. Above all, it is clear that effective ways for women and men to understand each other and lead together in the church have not yet emerged.

The Story of Advent Church

When Elizabeth became the new associate and the first woman pastor at Advent Church, she joined Bob, the senior pastor who was in his midfifties and had been at Advent for ten years; Jeff, the thirty-three-year-old education specialist/associate, who had been at Advent for a year; and the office staff assistants, Alice and Sandy. The staff also included Harold, sixty-three, who had served the congregation for twenty-one years as custodian. Elizabeth's arrival meant something to everyone in this group, and regardless of what they thought about her coming, they all worked hard to welcome her. It was a "new day" at Advent.

During the first week, Elizabeth learned many important things about the parish, the volunteer committees, the office procedures, the preaching schedule for the next few months, and the issues facing the congregation in the immediate future. In turn, the staff had a chance to get to know more about Elizabeth and what she would be doing in her specialty as music director/pastor. In the months that followed, Elizabeth learned a great deal more about the daily life of the congregation, the groups who used the building on weekdays, the life and work of the parish committees, the youth, the choirs, the worship schedule and liturgies, and, of course, the individual people and their concerns—so many things that are part of the routine of pastoring and caring for a congregation.

Elizabeth settled in. She was happy to be part of a team. In her first call, she had been alone in a very small parish. It had been lonely for a single woman. Then she had returned to graduate school to study church music. This made her a more attractive candidate for a team ministry and allowed her to enjoy her love of music. At Advent, she got off to a great start with the choirs and did many things to enhance the music programs of the congregation. She had her committee assignments, her visits to the sick and shut-ins, and all the routine tasks of an associate to keep her very busy. She got to know Sandy quite well, but noticed that Alice was aloof and a bit unfriendly in the office. Harold was polite but quiet and reserved around her while he seemed friendly and joked a lot with the other pastors. Jeff became a real friend, and Elizabeth came to know his wife and young children as well. They reminded her what a "pioneer" she was and told her how important it was for young women in the parish to see her as a role model. Bob was friendly too but, as senior pastor, he kept his distance from Elizabeth, as he had always done with Jeff.

It was great to be part of a team. Elizabeth liked Advent, the community, and the congregation. True, she never did understand why Bob continued to attend her committee meetings. The minor controversy that erupted in the senior choir when she tried to make some of the hymn language more inclusive was a discouraging setback. She was frustrated when the Committee for a New Organ didn't seem willing to take her recommendations without Bob's backing. She wondered why she could never get to know Alice very well, no matter how hard she tried, and she wished Harold would be as friendly with her as he was with the other pastors. Even Jeff's encouragement sometimes reminded her of the burden of being a role model for all the girls in the congregation.

But Elizabeth had grown used to these things. They were all part of being a woman in ministry. She could give her office work to Sandy and avoid dealing with Alice. She accepted the polite distance from Harold. She tried to be a good role model, spending extra time with the girls and boys in the congregation. She even designed a special music camp her first summer. It came off well, though both Bob and Jeff got frustrated about how much decision making Elizabeth let the volunteers do. In all, if anyone had asked Elizabeth and her colleagues how they got along, they probably all would have said, "We get along pretty well. It's a nice staff." And most members of the congregation would have said the same.

Then one day in staff meeting something happened that Elizabeth couldn't overlook. Bob shared the sermon schedule for the quarter and Elizabeth noticed that she had only one assignment, instead of the usual three or four. It seemed odd, but she didn't want to say anything right then. She'd think about it for awhile, and plan carefully how to approach Bob with her concern. She knew she should not discuss it with Jeff. The correct thing was to deal directly with Bob. Things got busy after that and by the time Elizabeth had a chance to talk to Bob, the quarter was almost over. It seemed like an old issue, and she decided to let it go. When the next quarter's schedule came out, Elizabeth still had only two Sundays to preach, and the holiday preaching was assigned to Bob and Jeff. She wanted to know why, but at the moment she was too upset to ask. She hesitated to create a scene with Bob, realizing that she was upset. In fact, she was angry.

Elizabeth's anger didn't go away; neither did her ambivalence about talking to Bob. Jeff noticed that she was testy after that day, and asked if anything was wrong. Elizabeth avoided the real issue. Finally, after a couple of weeks of tiptoeing around the office, both Jeff and Bob decided that something must be wrong. What was it? As senior pastor, Bob would have to find out.

Bob approached Elizabeth in a very matter-of-fact way, opening the door, he thought, to a brief clarifying discussion. Elizabeth asked him about the preaching with barely-controlled anger. She even shed a few tears before she was able to bring her emotions under control. She was hurt and angry, and she had let this go too long, she knew. Why, she asked, had Bob reduced her preaching assignments? And why didn't he know what she was upset about? He should have!

Bob was stunned by the force of Elizabeth's feelings. It was true, he had done it on purpose. He had heard concerns from both men and women in the congregation who said they just preferred having one of the men preach. Elizabeth had been hired primarily to take care of the music program anyway. Bob had seen no reason to discuss these matters with Elizabeth. It would only hurt her feelings. Besides, he did want to support her ministry. He wanted to advocate for women in the pastorate of this church by having one here. He was doing quite a bit, he thought. Why was she blowing up at him like this? And then of course, he was the senior pastor. He was responsible for making final decisions. No one had ever questioned his authority like this before. Anyway, it wasn't that big a deal—only one Sunday or two a quarter.

Bob and Elizabeth talked it through. They even brought Jeff into the discussion so all three would know what the issue was and how it had been resolved. Bob increased Elizabeth's preaching assignments the next quarter, but she noticed that he never assigned her to preach on a festival Sunday, and he did not assign her weddings and funerals unless parishioners specifically asked for her. Bob noticed that Elizabeth remained more aloof. They just didn't seem to get along as well. He wondered why and regretted it, but figured he couldn't do any more about it. He didn't want to create controversy within the parish. It was best left alone, he thought, best left alone.

Themes from Men and Women

The problems encountered by the staff at Advent Church illustrate many of the fourteen themes that emerged in interviews with women and men in leadership in Protestant churches. These themes summarize what they have to say about themselves and each other as leaders in the church. They also address what women say about the church as a place to be leaders with men.

THEME ONE: **Since women have entered church leadership in significant numbers, the acceptable styles of leadership have multiplied.** Though most church women agree that women bring new ways of leadership to the workplace and demonstrate some clearly identifiable skills, they are reluctant to conclude that women "have a unique style." They are reluctant to stereotype, and they raise articulate and thoughtful cautions about women's style that can only be answered by more time, more observation, and the presence of more women in leadership.

THEME TWO: **Women in leadership must compromise.** There is no way around it. Because the workplace is defined and controlled by men, women's ways of leading are often misunderstood and rendered ineffective. Often, women have to compromise their preferred style for one that works in the prevailing paradigm. Furthermore, even though they cannot avoid compromises, women are uncomfortable in revealing them. They wish they did not have to make them. They feel sometimes angry, sometimes ashamed, sometimes intensely private about them. For this reason, as well as others, women are often very cautious about disclosing interior motivations. They request anonymity. They emphasize the desire to speak not as victims but as legitimate

leaders whose style or contributions are not always noticed or rewarded.

THEME THREE: Women get a mixed message from the church.
Because of quotas or just because the churches have "put out the call"
for women leaders, women in the established denominations hear a
message of welcome. The church is more open than the corporate
world to women and more pro-active in providing leadership roles and
positions for women. But at the same time, the church remains a
fundamentally male hierarchy. Once inside, women get another message entirely. They find that they are not so welcome after all. The
ways in which women get this message are complex and subtle. Men
may not know to what extent women get a mixed message.

Furthermore, in some evangelical denominations women are not
welcomed into leadership. They do not hear the call at all, or they are
called to leadership with restrictions. Finally, the debate about quotas
notwithstanding, the numbers alone show that most women, regardless of denomination, do not have access to leadership in the same way
that men do.

**THEME FOUR: In the patriarchal environment of the denomina-
tions, theology and language work against women.** Traditionally
theology has been derived systematically in the male style. Until
recently, the very nature of the theological enterprise has been based
on white male ideas and experience. Certainly there's been no room
for women's experience. Orthodox (i.e., male) theologies also incorporate patriarchal notions of the supremacy of the male, making sexism
appear the normative nature of human relations. Furthermore, an
oppressive interpretation of the theology of Paul has been used against
women in very specific ways. The result: for women, the truth of the
gospel has long been threatened by theologies and practices that
legitimize men's domination over them. Furthermore, women have
not felt the freedom to think theologically in their own style, until very
recently.

Language also works against women. In a patriarchy, our language
about God persists in reflecting a man-God. As a result, we think of
God as male—and even think of the male as more like God than the
female. Ordinary language also works against women. Our rules for

using masculine pronouns remind us constantly that men are active in human history. Women are less visible, sometimes invisible. In these and other ways, language keeps women in a one-down position.

THEME FIVE: Women work as immigrants in a foreign land. Even in the church, which is in many ways a more welcoming environment for them than the corporate world, women do not know the language or culture, and they are often trapped in difficult situations that they cannot interpret. This dilemma is exponentially compounded for women who are not white and of northern European extraction. Men often do not know that women are immigrants; they assume that ambitious female leaders know the culture.

THEME SIX: Issues of invisibility are the most common traps for women. When asked about traps that catch them, women most readily and most frequently cite the invisibility traps. They recall frequent instances of having their ideas ignored or taken over by men. They often realize that they are ignored or completely overlooked in meetings. Sometimes, they become so obviously a token that they are visible only as females, not as competent coworkers. These are the experiences of invisibility. They are so routine that women accept them, unhappily, as a normal part of their work life.

THEME SEVEN: Women in leadership burn out quickly. This is not because they have more family concerns than men do. It is because they must work very hard and they cannot count on rewards for doing so. In fact, they may be punished for working hard and doing well, because their success makes men uncomfortable. A contributing factor is that family concerns are still seen as primarily theirs. They are not shared equally by men.

THEME EIGHT: Women feel unsafe because their physical boundaries are routinely compromised. This does not happen just in dark alleys or parking lots. It happens in the workplace, even in the church. Some of the ways in which this happens are not obvious and are not discussed. Harassment is the red flag everyone is waving these days, but women are also violated by constant scrutiny of their appearance, and the difficulty they face in "just being themselves" in the workplace.

THEME NINE: In striving to work successfully with women, men are trapped too. They are trapped by stereotypes, by an entrenched hierarchy, by their own fears, by women's emotional reactions, by their own tendency to take charge, and by the reputation they have as "jerks." Women don't always know what these traps are, but they are aware of men's struggle to work with them. They know that "men feel the pain too."

THEME TEN: There are tasks for women and tasks for men. Men's tasks come first. Men are in control of the workplace world. Economics and a wish for a fuller life have brought women into that world. But within the prevailing paradigm, men are still very much in control. They have the power and the influence. They know and make the rules of the culture. They therefore have a primary responsibility to advocate for and nurture the success of women. Women have important tasks too. Unless men undertake their tasks seriously, however, what women do will not make much difference. There is general recognition among both women and men that men have primary responsibility here.

THEME ELEVEN: Women want men to listen. The response is overwhelming and clear. Women emphasized that they do not want men to do something. First, and most important, they want men to listen. And they added, they know this is not a natural "first thing" for men to do. But men need to listen, because real change must come from them if any change is going to be effective.

THEME TWELVE: Childhood experience teaches men how to work with women. Men say that the one thing that most prepares them to work effectively with women is the influence of strong women in their early lives, especially their mothers. Similar female role models later in life have a positive impact, the men report, but are not as formative for them as women in their youth. Men share this response almost without exception.

THEME THIRTEEN: Women are ambivalent about power. They have trouble claiming their power and speaking from their own position of power. They reject the way men have traditionally used power for a number of different and complex reasons. Sometimes, it does not occur to them that power in itself is not bad, but that the abuse of power is. As a result of their ambivalence about power, women often speak from a position of weakness. They sound like victims even though they do not want to be victims. They want to tell their stories, and they may not know how to do so in a powerful way.

THEME FOURTEEN: Women need mentoring. They need mentoring from men, who can show them how to survive in a male-centered workplace. They also need mentoring from other women, who can help them "stay on course," remaining true to their own style of leading in an environment that is not always friendly or appreciative of their style. Furthermore, women ask for mentoring with the assumption that men already get it from one another. In other words, women assume that men get mentored in the church just as they do in the business world, whether or not this is true.

An Ordinary Tale

There is nothing shocking or unusual about the story of Advent Church and its staff. The things that happened there are typical of what happens frequently to women and men working together in church leadership. It is a composite, fictionalized account[1] based on real-life anecdotes from women and men who work in the church, not only as clergy, but as lay professionals and as volunteers. The first important characteristic of this story is that it is so ordinary. What happened to Elizabeth and Bob and Jeff, and the others at Advent isn't unusual. It happens all the time—so often that it's expected. It's routine. It's the way things are. In the chapters that follow, we shall hear many other true stories that illustrate these themes.

They are ordinary stories, too, but what they show us is not always obvious. The situation of women and men working together in church leadership seems so clear when we describe it in a list and so much more subtle when experienced. It's easy to consider the list of themes above and to say, "Oh yes, I know about that!" In practice, as at Advent, the interplay of the themes is often much more subtle and unclear. The themes are harder to name and understand when they are part of a lived experience. Women may tend to notice the things that go wrong because they are sensitized. Still, it's possible for both women and men working in partnerships all over the church to be so much "inside of " a situation that they don't notice or can't articulate what's wrong.

A lot of things did go wrong at Advent Church. It wasn't that the staff got off to the wrong start. In fact, they did many things right in the beginning. No matter how hard they all worked, however, the staff at Advent never really got to know one another as men and women working together. Bob didn't realize that he was "walking on eggshells" when Elizabeth got mad and wouldn't say anything. Elizabeth didn't know that it was better to be direct and clear, and that Bob would not expect her to give his feelings much thought in her decision about how to confront him. Bob didn't know that he was taking over when he cut Elizabeth's preaching assignments. Elizabeth didn't know that Bob was uncertain about her leadership because she deferred decisions to others too often. Bob didn't anticipate that Elizabeth would be viewed with discomfort by many parishioners, especially when she got in the pulpit. And neither one of them knew that the other was uncertain and even scared about their shared ministry.

With their common lack of knowledge and their inability to truly acknowledge one another, the staff of Advent Church blundered into trouble. Bob wanted to advocate for women in ministry and was open to a woman associate, especially when the call committee approved of Elizabeth and advocated for her with the congregation. Still, he didn't want to have any controversy in the parish over her ministry. Jeff supported her as much as he could, but felt powerless when relationships began to simmer and boil. Bob was the senior pastor, and he had always made that clear to both Jeff and Elizabeth. Harold thought Elizabeth was a nice enough young woman, but he wondered quietly to himself what this world was coming to, that we had to have women pastors. Alice didn't like it at all, this young woman coming into the parish and taking over. Who did she think she was? Before she came, Alice always had more influence with Bob. Sandy was just Sandy, delighted to have Elizabeth and not sure what all the fuss was about. Elizabeth was overwhelmed trying to be a perfect role model and fit into a staff that she couldn't always figure out.

Elizabeth's advent at Advent did not change anyone or anything. The team disintegrated because the people didn't know how to work together. The men did not know anything about the special concerns of women in leadership. They did not realize that Elizabeth might go about her work in a different way than they expected. They were unaware of how others in the congregation might react to their first female pastor. Nor did they understand their responsibility to help themselves, Elizabeth, and the congregation make a successful transition to having a woman as pastor. Elizabeth, on the other hand, had few real clues about how to work as a minority person in an unfamiliar culture. She didn't know how to relate to the men: how they would tend to think, address tasks, get things done. In their world, she didn't know the rules.

These problems, working together subtly, undermined the leadership of each pastor at Advent Church before anyone really understood what was happening and, as a result, destroyed the partnerships they had with one another. That's what happens when you don't really know where you're going or how to get there or who the strangers are who are on the road with you. Alice found that out in Wonderland. Elizabeth learned it at Advent Church.

Chapter Two

Women Leading
in the Church

One activity that church leaders engage in on a regular basis is the planning and executing of large group meetings. Fran and Gary work for different congregations, but both have participated in this activity. Fran is a senior supervisor who has been responsible for overall planning of such events for her denomination. In Gary's denomination, Gary's boss is responsible for the planning of similar meetings. Gary has carried out assignments in preparation for these gatherings for three different bosses—two men, and currently a woman. Here's what Fran and Gary have to say about their experience.

Gary: I play a significant part in planning the assembly because I am responsible for the operation of the plenary hall. Each time we have done more and more, to the point that I oversee the whole thing. I sit in on all the committees. When I worked for George, our planning meetings were not long and mainly we'd get ideas and would go off and work on them and touch base with one another as we went. I'd meet with him privately and we'd go over the things that needed to be done so that I would do my things and he would do his, and everything got taken care of. When Linda became my boss, the committee became more integral. So it just took longer. There were times I was just climbing the walls because I was so task-oriented and decision-driven. I was ready to say, "OK, we decided this, let's go on," or "OK, we've got to quit talking and make the decision and go on." But it just went on and on. After a couple of years, when there were more women on the committee—all of them capable, competent, and strong like Linda—we refined the process to a fine art. But it seemed to me that we planned the event 250 times over!

Fran: It seemed that way to you, but how did it seem to them?

Gary: For them, I think each time was progress and each time was building and refining and strengthening. They were thinking of all the parts as a whole, planning the event that way.

Fran: That causes me to reflect on what happens with our events. Because now that I am in charge of them, my whole perspective is, what kind of experience is the individual person going to have there?

Gary: That's what I mean. I think that's the way Linda works, too.

Fran: I never thought about it, really. I do know that other people—especially men—get frustrated. For some of them, their perspective is, "What business has to be completed here?" You see? I don't tend to think in those terms. I think about the whole experience, and we have radically changed the experience that people have, but we haven't necessarily changed the way business is concluded.

Gary: Yes, and the only reason I had the patience for the process was because I counted on the Holy Spirit being there, especially in the beginning when I was skeptical. Eventually I did recognize what the women were trying to do.

Fran: How did you recognize it?

Gary: Even I, task-oriented as I am, recognize the importance of process and focus. But that's not where I normally start. What I tend to do is look at what we want to have happen and ask what are the pieces that have to be put together to take care of that, and what is the order, and let's get on with it and let's not do all this talking.

Fran: I'm not uncomfortable with the process, but I know some of the men in our group are. How do the women feel in your situation?

Gary: Not only does it not bother them . . . I hadn't thought about this before . . . but the process develops leadership in the church almost as much as the event itself.

Fran: If you observe the way women's organizations in all the denominations work, that is also true. The process of bringing people into leadership and moving them from one leadership position to another actually develops leadership, and these women's groups as a whole raise millions of dollars for ministry.

Church Women and Their Style

A **process orientation** is one characteristic of the style that churchwomen describe as important. In the preceding dialogue, note that Fran valued the process as much as the product. "I am a process person," says one woman, "One of my strengths is in involving people in the decision-making process. This may be self-serving in that I enjoy the process and the gathering of information. But I see myself as good at getting people together to gather information. My ego is fed by the process we go through, no matter what the task is. If *how we got there* was good for me and for everybody else, if people are feeling good and everyone is excited, that is much better than if we get there and I had to force everybody." She gets people to engage in process, she says, "by inviting them into the discussion, and sharing my energy. Nobody can get motivated if they can't understand why the train is going in a certain direction."

THEME ONE: Since women have entered church leadership in significant numbers, the acceptable styles of leadership have multiplied.

A part of this concern for process comes from a woman's wish to see the task holistically. Both Linda and Fran, the congregational leaders in charge of planning events, have a **focus on the whole experience.** Other women share this concern as well. "Women have a more holistic style generally," one observes. "Our society really encourages men to work for achievement and job success, and there are certain things that they have to do to climb the ladder. Women have not been raised that way or socialized into that kind of understanding about how leadership works."

Many church women also highlight **participatory management** as a cornerstone of their style. "Women just tend to do a
lot more collaborative leadership than individual decision making," says one. "It's not that they can't make the final decision.
It's just that they get a lot more input prior to making the
decision." Another adds, "I always consult. I'm fairly decisive,
but I test my decisions with others and try to get participation
and ownership." A pastor doing new ministry development col-
laborates by having an advisory council. "I work better in coun-
sel, in trying to listen to other people's perspectives and
ultimately . . . making the decision." Another veteran of volunteer positions says, "I like to build consensus. That's my primary
style." An executive characterized this trait in women as "the
willingness to spend time with people creating win-win situations." "It's really an empowerment model," a young executive
agrees. She is embarking on an inquiry process with staff and
partner churches to determine future directions for the agency
she heads.

This tendency to work for consensus does not mean that women
cannot make decisions. In fact, the women interviewed were quick to
point this out. One woman amplifies: "My style is to bring together
everybody as often as possible to have input," she says, but she does
not use consensus style. "Nothing ever gets decided that way. What
people really want is somebody to provide leadership, gather input,
and then make the decisions." That's what she does. "It's really up to
me to decide, but they all get a say, and it becomes much more of a
group process. I try to balance getting input and making decisions
when necessary."

A veteran volunteer in church work summarizes it this way: "Very
seldom do you find a woman who wants to be in control and not take
other things into consideration. She will listen. Women can listen to
everything. They can make decisions. They can also be objective and
sort through what the problems are, what the challenges and goals are,
and then come up with what they feel is necessary. But at the same
time, they are team players." Another professional laywoman in the
service of the church adds this: "We've learned how to collaborate and
what that means. I get something; you get something; and we all get
something in return."

A part of collaborative leadership is the **willingness to share information,** churchwomen say. "Women don't see leadership as having to have all the answers and be the expert. At least I don't. My responsibility is to find the information and make it possible for that information to come forward and become a part of our process," says one church agency director. Part of our struggle is that we're often expected to operate from a top-down position. We aren't comfortable there. We don't necessarily want to be there. It's isolated, lonely, and frustrating there. We see ourselves in the middle of concentric circles rather than at the top of the ladder. It's a totally different power position. It's a sharing of power, a sharing of authority, a sharing of vision. In order to work this way, you can't view power as finite. Women come out of an empowerment model that says if we share power, we all have more. Men don't get that." Another manager of a church-related agency takes this philosophy so seriously that she has no middle management in her staff. "Everybody reports to me. That's nearly twenty people, and that's a lot to manage, but they all need access to me." Both of these women are considered very successful in their work by their peers, both women and men.

Very closely related to the ability to collaborate is the **ability to negotiate.** "I happen to think that in all the jobs I have had, it's been extremely important to be able to negotiate," says one woman who has had a long career in church volunteer and professional posts. This comes, she says, from a fundamental commitment to collaborative work with others and a willingness to go for the win-win solution. It requires many of the traits we've already discussed—openness, sharing information, flexibility, and a commitment to solve problems with people.

All of these skills come from a woman's fundamental **concern for human relationships,** churchwomen say. "We bring a more relational approach to leadership. We are much more concerned about preserving relationships than men are," said one clergywoman. "Women generally have been brought up to take care of relationships, and I think women clergy are no different than other women in this way." One church administrator explains her own approach to relationships this way: "I interact with people on a relationship level long before they have to carry out any orders I might issue. I first work on the relationship and what that person most wants to do in his or her job."

Aren't men concerned about relationships too? "Absolutely not," she says. "Little boys are not raised to focus on the finer points of relationships. Little girls are, because that's how you are supposed to get a man!"

Women comment on how much time they spend at work caring for people and their concerns. This they consider to be vital to making sure that the work gets done and done well. Men, they say, don't always agree, but that may be because the women are doing the task for them. On the other hand, says one clergywoman, it may be that men are more willing to let relationships go.[1] "Women spend most of their time making sure their relationships are good. Working relationships are very important to them, and I don't think they are as important to men."

The closeness that women feel toward other people may assist them in **bringing intimacy to the workplace,** some say. "I have what a lot of managers would probably call an informal style. My door is always open, whereas a lot of other managers here call their own people into their office rather than walking over to see them," says an administrator. By virtue of their informality, "women bring a certain intimacy to the workplace that may be the single thing that makes men most uncomfortable," another offers, and many agreed with her. "By that I mean a kind of personal style—less academic, less absolute."

Their domestic roles provide women leaders with another valuable skill. "By virtue of their life experience, women tend to be able to **do many things at once,**" suggests one, who in her own case attributes this skill to mothering. "Motherhood is a good way to prepare for a lot of jobs because you have to take care of competing claims, deal with a lot of egos and, sometimes, a lot of serious demands. You have to take one problem at a time and solve it and not become overwhelmed with what could seem like unsolvable problems." A clergywoman puts it more graphically: "If you run a halfway decent household, you get up in the morning and you've got fourteen projects going on, and they all have to end at 3:30 when the kids get home . . . the cake in the oven, the laundry, and everything else. You learn time management. You learn attention to detail." This pastor has learned to call upon women volunteers, she says, "when I need forty-seven letters sent, flowers on the tables, and all kinds of other arrangements made all at once." But for the single tasks, especially if they require public visibility, she often finds the men more willing.

Finally, and perhaps the most critical for their survival in the male paradigm, these women are **risk takers.** "My style is to do my homework, to listen to others, but at the same time, I stick by my principles. I'm not afraid to take the risk," says one long-time volunteer. "I look to be innovative whenever I take on an assignment, and if I don't feel I can make a real contribution, I'll say no," she adds.

A clergywoman building new ministries agrees, "I am a risk taker, very much so. I look at things by asking: What have we got to lose? The worst anybody can say is no. But I'm not afraid to take that risk because it gets contagious and people begin to imagine what ministry can be like." She's broken some barriers as a result. "Without being conscious of it, people have an idea of what leadership is supposed to look like, and it's a man. And it's supposed to be done according to a particular idea they had in mind. Once, when I presented an idea to my bishop he said, 'Do you realize that this would mean we'd have to change our whole way of doing mission?' I just said, 'Well, I really think it's what we should do.' And eventually we did."

A bishop sums it up this way: "You have to have some core beliefs and you have to have a vision [about] where you are headed." With this clear, she says, "You have to be willing to risk losing face. You can't lead if you are not prepared to have people hate you. You must be willing to have your reputation go completely down the river. Standing for something. That's leadership."

Is Women's Style Unique? What Women Say

Letty Russell challenges women "to look for clues about what feminist leadership gifts . . . might look like. We will most certainly not expect any one model or task to emerge, but it seems we could expect a particular style of leadership behavior with clues or indications that the empowerment of authority in community is already beginning to happen."[2] This is exactly what women in church leadership are doing as they articulate their own style. They are searching alone and together for ways of articulating that style. Whether or not they have a unique style is far less important to them than knowing what their style is, valuing it, and having it validated in the workplace. And to be sure, "until women's wisdom . . . is infused into our cultural institutions . . . we will be bereft of the wisdom we need to change our ways. . . . We ask women [therefore] to learn their histories; not just their personal histories but their cultural histories."[3]

There is significant evidence in the descriptions provided by church women that they do have different styles of leadership than men. Despite all the evidence that women themselves provide about the uniqueness of their leadership style, however, we must be cautious. There are several concerns that the women themselves raise. First, these women, like all thoughtful people, are reluctant to stereotype. They don't want to be trapped in a new sexism, "the bleary-eyed idea that women's natural gifts . . . make her ideally suited to ministry."[4] They are reluctant to say that "women are one way" and "men are another" because one can always find the exceptions. As we shall see in the development of this book, the church has more than its share of exceptions to the idea that men are hierarchical and authoritarian in their leadership.[5] There are also exceptions to the idea that women are embracing or collaborative.

Second, women hesitate to claim their differences, lest these be used against them. As we shall see, women have good reason to fear this outcome. Differences do get used very effectively against women in the church, though they should not be. This fact is the result of our stubbornly dualistic thinking.

A third and most compelling caution is the possibility that women's style is culturally conditioned and enforced by the expectations of both men and women. In fact, if it were not so, perhaps women's leadership styles would vary more than they do. We cannot know, of course, what women's styles might be if our cultural paradigms were different.[6] But we can look at how women's style may be predictable based on the prevailing paradigm of the white male system. A simpler way of saying this is: perhaps women are relational, collaborative, process oriented, informal, and problem solving in their leadership *because they are expected to be that way.*

One woman puts it this way: "I think women are only allowed one leadership style. It's curious. There just isn't a lot of room for diversity of styles yet." If women are assertive, goal-directed, firm, even authoritative, they may be criticized for being bitchy or tough or unfeminine. Perhaps, then, they rely on a style that is more acceptable within the prevailing paradigm. Women themselves contribute to this dilemma. "Female staff always approach me much more personally, much more intimately than the men do. They expect me to be closer to them." Paradoxically, she adds, "That need to collapse the distance that *should* exist between me and the staff is sometimes an urge on my part as well as theirs." As a result, she says, she and other women in leadership do not have the same chances to establish the authority and credibility that they need in order to be recognized by men and to work successfully in a man's world. Women must have that chance, says another, "because there is still a tendency for a woman in leadership not to be accepted at the same level as a man."

Women are also ambivalent about power and, therefore, uncertain about using it themselves. This adds to the difficulty of being any other kind of leader but collaborative. "I try to be the nicest boss I possibly can be, even to the point of doing menial tasks because I too have done my time [as a secretary] jumping up when the bell rang and running into the [male] boss's office. I hated it," recalls one woman with still discernible passion in her voice. Women with memories like this have a very difficult time embracing power. They have legitimate reason to be ambivalent about it.

One professor recounts facing this dilemma when writing a syllabus for a class on power with another female professor. "We didn't want to use the typical passive voice, which masks who's doing the requiring and therefore who has the power. We wanted to name who has the power in the class. But we couldn't bring ourselves to do it in an autocratic way either, legislating and mandating course work. We had to find language somewhere in between. We wanted to acknowledge our authority as the professors without being hierarchical."

Are women collaborative, then, because they are expected to be, because they are repulsed by the way the power of the hierarchical model has been used against them and their sisters (and their minority brothers), or because they really are collaborative leaders? It's probably "all of the above." We cannot know until more women have been in leadership for a longer time.

Another way to look at this issue is to view how women have led in the last few generations. Women and men nearing retirement report that those few women of their generation or previous generations who made it into leadership were successful by imitating the male paradigm—in the hierarchical model. They surmise this was because so few women were in leadership, and there was really no other acceptable way. Now, with more women in leadership, we can see the emergence of a style like we have described in this chapter.[7]

Whether or not women have a unique style of leadership may not be clear. Obviously, however, the presence of more and more women in leadership has opened up the styles that are acceptable for both women and men. The title of "senior minister" is fading for many congregations. Observes one woman: "What you are pointing to in your question [about styles] is that men and women are really beginning to change one another as they become partners in the workplace. I think one of the major changes [in the church] is exactly that partnership." She points particularly to congregations who are able to move to "shared leadership . . . and find themselves served well by partners."[8] She adds, "Young men particularly are finding this not only to be an attractive style, but somewhat of a relief." No longer do they have to be the authority all the time. Another clergywoman puts it more bluntly. Men have to work more relationally, she says, "because women are making them."

Women agree that they must forge ways of leading that are unique, regardless of how their style is described. This is difficult because they are defined as leaders in relation to men and men's style.[9] "It's unfortunate that the only model we have is the male model," says one woman pastor. "So, of course, that's the one we think is best to be like. When we begin to be successful, we begin to act like them, and it's not natural." Women have to be unique, she stresses, "because men will never accept us, no matter how much we become like them. If we could just be all right with who we are and do that to the maximum . . . but I wonder if we know who we are. Our roles have been too defined by men" for us to know ourselves.

This candid comment summarizes the dilemma for women. Women know that they are outsiders. No matter what they do, their experience has taught them that they are not "one of the guys." They know they will never be accepted in that way, and furthermore, they aren't sure they want to be. Still, they are defined by a male standard. The imperative to be known as unique and valuable is crucial for them.[10]

"We are just learning how to use our own strength" in leadership, says one female pastor. "We are learning how to do it because we have to do it differently than men." Another woman's comment illustrates how women can learn from men *but ought to use that information as women*: "We do need to learn some of the positive strategies that men know," she says, "but we have to do that in a situation where we are sharing that information with each other as women."

Chapter Three

Leadership Paradigms and Women as Leaders

When women move into leadership positions in the church they receive many mixed messages about themselves and their work.

A middle-level manager in a major denomination was recently up for a promotion to senior management, a measure that had to be approved by the denomination's Board of Directors. Her supervisor told her in advance that he would recommend her, and, indeed, she did receive the promotion. But immediately after the board meeting, the supervisor called her to his office to report that "a substantial number of board members had voted against her reappointment." The supervisor surmised this was in part because she was "too aggressive." When the woman objected, citing examples of her male colleagues who were far more aggressive in similar situations, the supervisor readily agreed. He even sympathized. But he added, "That's just the way things are."

For a half dozen years or more, a lay woman working in campus ministry carried out a successful and well-respected ministry. She received affirmation from pastors and other leaders in her denomination for her success in a unique and challenging university setting. In 1991, she decided to seek ordination and turned to her congregation, which, in her denomination, approves and carries out ordinations. What followed was a major controversy between the leadership and the membership of the congregation. The deacons of her congregation "were uncomfortable ordaining a woman," so they offered her "partial ordination" instead. The members of the congregation overruled the deacons and the controversy heated up. Eventually, the woman joined a different congregation in order to be ordained without controversy, but this only angered the leadership in her former setting. This woman is now ordained, but the controversy surrounding her remains. She still faces the real possibility that she will lose her job as a result, and she has also been the target of harassment and other personal threats during the controversy, which has lasted several years.

These scenarios illustrate at least three mixed messages, all of which are confusing to thoughtful women. First of course is the compelling message that women long to hear from the church: "We want you here. We know you have something to contribute. We want to bless your special leadership gifts on behalf of the church." The second message is a bit more problematic, and goes something like this: "If you are going to be here, we want you to act in a way that will be comfortable for us (men)." The implication of this second message for the intelligent woman is, of course, that the men aren't really sure that they *do* want her there after all. But the third message is the real clincher. It's simple: "This is the way things are (in these examples, women aren't supposed to be aggressive, or too powerful, or too visible) and you have to fit in." This message makes no sense to women because it does not fit the paradigm out of which they live and work.

Paradigms, Women, and Men

A paradigm is a set of deeply held rules and regulations surrounding the way people see and do things; it provides boundaries for us. We use paradigms to filter information, to make sense of our world, and to help us decide how to do the things we do.[1] We use paradigms in this way as individuals, as groups, and in entire organizations. Even the church relies on paradigms in this way.

In the medieval period, people thought that the earth was flat, with a sky canopy overhead containing the stars, the moon, planets, and above all, heaven, the realm of divine substance. People feared that going to the edge of the world would mean falling off into "outer darkness," or hell.[2] The church embraced this paradigm, and held the loyalty of the people by conjuring up images of all manner of monsters who lurked around the dark edges of the flat earth. Staying in the center of the world, which was also believed to be the center of the universe, was safest.

The idea that the earth was the center of the universe persisted despite the pioneering scientific work of Copernicus in the early sixteenth century, and in the next century, Galileo. Eventually the published treatises of Galileo and the work of Newton, which built upon it, put an end to that paradigm. It took 150 years for the old paradigm to break down. Copernicus himself had been afraid to publish his heliocentric theories, and with good reason.[3] When Galileo perfected the theory and published in 1632, he was reviled and condemned by the church for his trouble. Only in 1992 did the Roman Catholic church officially recant his condemnation. It's shocking now for us to remember this example. It seems ludicrous that the church fathers reacted so violently against Galileo, who was, after all, correct.

A paradigm is also a conceptual trap if we can't see beyond it. It is like a black hole in space. Once inside, there seems to be no way out. It is "like a room which—once inside—you cannot imagine a world outside."[4] It's not surprising, therefore that "people who create new paradigms are outsiders."[5] (Galileo, and later Newton, surely were!) They also are not very well accepted and their ideas or their actions are rejected. The first people to adopt a new paradigm must be very courageous.[6] We know that from Copernicus and his followers. Still, we forget it when we revile the paradigm shifters or busters of our own day.

There are many examples of paradigm shifts in our own day. Christianity itself provides us with one. The church has lost influence so swiftly in our secularized society that some observers believe it must fundamentally change in order to survive.[7] Our *paradigm* for the church must change. What the church as an institution does to help propagate the faith must be different fundamentally. Leaders in the church, both men and women, are reacting strongly, with fear, anger, excitement, and uncertainty. We have yet to see what will happen. But part of the reason we are afraid is that we cannot yet "see" the new paradigm. We are still in the old one.

Paradigms have everything to do with women in church leadership because the prevailing paradigm of our culture is the white male system. Ann Wilson Schaef first articulated this paradigm from a woman's point of view in 1981.[8] The myth this system perpetuates is that "reality is hierarchical."[9] "It is the system by which we live, and in it, the power and influence are held by white males. It controls almost

> *THEME TWO:*
> *Women in*
> *leadership must*
> *compromise.*

every aspect of our culture. It makes our laws, runs our economy, sets our salaries, and decides when and if we will go to war or stay at home. It decides what is knowledge, and how it will be taught."[10]

From one clergywoman's point of view, the prevailing paradigm "tells me over and over again that men are different from me, that culture sides with men in what it values, and that sometimes it is willing to be extremely mean, if not violent, toward me and other women to get what it wants." She adds: "I, of course, have this theory packed in my bags when I approach ministry and the doing of it."[11]

Like any other paradigm, the white male system can be changed. Still, as the prevailing paradigm of our culture, it's hard to remember that it is only one way of viewing the world. Like the medieval view of the universe that so powerfully ruled the imagination of the people in 1500, the white male system today holds us in its grasp. That is the nature of a prevailing paradigm. As every woman and man, black or white, Asian or Hispanic, or any other race knows, "there is a direct correlation between buying into the white male system and surviving in our culture."[12] What the paradigm misses is that outsiders (women, African Americans, Hispanic people and others) are not "additions to" or "defections from" the standard, but "elements of that life" with their own contributions that invade the prevailing paradigm.[13]

Letty Russell reminds us that the prevailing white male paradigm is patriarchal and "places everything in a hierarchy of domination and subordination, accepting the marginalization of the powerless as given." This paradigm "is a manifestation of a social system that changes form but continues to define women as marginal to the male center." Women and minority people of both genders are reacting. For one thing, they will no longer let talk about God, about themselves, and about the church continue in this patriarchal framework. As leaders in their own right, they will talk back to the church, to challenge the prevailing paradigm. Their back talk will be startling "because the voices doing the talking [are] not those of church officials and scholars, who are the usual interpreters of meaning in the church." They will often be the voices of women. This is appropriate. Talking back to the church is an accepted task of ecclesiology.[14]

Schaef and Russell, a psychologist and theologian respectively, are among a growing number of female authors who have begun to show us that gender issues are not to be taken *a priori*: "Organizations are not genderless in and of themselves," but in fact, reflect and contribute to the prevailing paradigm.[15] But if we can't "see" the paradigm "the prevalence of male experience and interpretation" is accepted as normative even though it is "exclusive of much of women's experience."[16]

The best way to see a paradigm clearly is to get outside of it, by putting ourselves into another one. Annie Machisale-Musopole, a writer and member of the Church of Central Africa-Presbyterian gives us an opportunity to do that by viewing the Chewa culture of her country. Here, women were traditionally seen as the source of the community's life and of communication with God. As such, they were accorded the highest religious respect. They were the prophets and religious leaders, and it was through images of woman that the people understood God. This was the prevailing religious paradigm of the Chewa. When the Western missionaries came, women were made slaves, and the paradigm was broken by the intervention of another culture.[17] But the paradigm was as legitimate as any other; it was a community's "shared way of understanding and interpreting reality," with a "common interpretive framework for what constitutes authority."[18] This example starkly illustrates that the notion of the church as an organization (or any organization's structure) "as an objective, empirical, and genderless reality" is itself a gendered notion. In a structure where male dominance is taken for granted, the assumption of the invisibility of gender can be understood as an ideological position.[19]

If paradigms help us sort and interpret information, they also help us make judgments, and it is here that they affect women in leadership today. We judge women competent or incompetent leaders based on our paradigm for leadership. If we accept the prevailing white male system as our paradigm (and, because it is the prevailing paradigm, most of us do to some degree), we are likely to find women wanting in their leadership, no matter what they do. A laywoman who has served her whole career with the church observes, "Women have to know how men think and what the male culture is. Whether or not they buy into it, they have to know what it is. Otherwise, they can't function." Even when they know the male culture, however, women are in a bind, as a clergywoman illustrates. "Men are graded on how well they do ministry the masculine way, and women are graded on how well they do it in the masculine way *as long as they also remain feminine*," she says.[20] If on the other hand, we can at least understand that there is a different paradigm operative for women, we will judge them differently.

A Woman's Paradigm for Leadership

Women do have different paradigms for leadership. Recent studies verify what churchwomen have said in chapter 2 about their leadership style. Judy Rosener hails a new generation of women leaders emerging in top management "not by adopting the style and habits that have proved successful for men, but by drawing on the skills and attitudes they developed from their shared experience as women." They are succeeding, observers say, "because of—not in spite of—certain characteristics generally considered to be 'feminine' and inappropriate in leaders."[21] Many authors observing both the secular and the religious leadership spheres characterize the leadership style of this new breed of women as *interactive* because they "encourage participation, share power and information, enhance other people's self worth, and get others excited about their work." Men, of course can work by these principles. Some actually do. Jesus' own ministry illustrates this point. In order to emulate Jesus' style, men must have healthy feminine aspects.[22]

Sally Helgesen pictures women as weavers. It is not so much the goal reached that is the point of satisfaction for women in leadership, she points out. It is as much the connections and the process used to reach the goals. And in making connections, women weave a "web of inclusion" in the workplace. The point of authority in the web is the heart, not the head. In "emphasizing interrelationships, working to tighten them, building up strength, knitting loose ends into the fabric, it is a strategy that honors the feminine principles of inclusion, connection" and it "betrays the female's essential orientation toward process, her concern with the means used to achieve her ends." The creation of the web is guided by opportunity, proceeds by the use of intuition, and is characterized by a patience that comes from waiting to see what comes next.[23] These are principles for leadership that come more naturally to women, because they come from the feminine within us.

Other observers concur. Deborah Tannen's language analysis shows that the goal of men in conversation is power, whereas for women, it is establishing relationships.[24] In comparing women's style to the dominant white male paradigm, Schaef describes male managers typically as "being in front," having the information and the answers, presenting an all-knowing image, and female system leaders as facilitators—finding people, nudging them, encouraging.[25] Women bring a balance to the workplace, tending to work as consensus managers rather than tough leaders.[26] Recent studies in women's psychology point to evidence that women leaders are less interested in competition and "beating others," as a mark of their achievement, and in fact "seem to combine traditional characteristics of both sexes, incorporating not only traditionally masculine aspects of achievement orientation, but also an inclination to nurturance and to value relationships."[27]

As we have already seen, women working in the church demonstrate these differences just as much as women in the corporation. They want power in order to share with others and get the job done by collaboration. They may have trouble accepting their own power and acting powerfully, as men do, but "because their bodies give them graceful lessons in letting happen what needs to happen, women sometimes show a paradoxical strength as they embrace their vulnerability."[28] Men, on the other hand, tend to want to act powerfully in order to influence others, and they may avoid their vulnerability. In the woman's paradigm for leadership, "power is something to be multiplied and shared rather than accumulated at the top." Women in leadership "indicate an intention, not simply to reverse the paradigm of domination, but to search out an alternative way of ordering our reality and world." The task for women is to determine "how to be a feminist leader in a patriarchal world."[29]

Fundamental to the feminine approach is experience. Tied closely to experience, of course, are relationships, process, change, interaction, and waiting. If there is a style of leadership more characteristic of women, it may be called "embracing," whereas a man's style may be characterized as "standing firm."[30]

These "embracing" qualities are the very principles of leadership that are increasingly affirmed in management literature, by Total Quality Management, by the call for more team building in management, by relational management, and by the churches' biblical models for leadership that are nurtured among the laity. Such affirmation predicts that the principles of the "embracing" paradigm should be legitimized as an important component of effective leadership, especially in the church. As this happens, the white male system should give way to a more integrated model of leadership that will embody the best of what both the "standing firm" and the "embracing" styles have to offer.[31] Women hope this will happen in the church. When it does, they hope their contributions to leadership will be recognized.

Revisiting the Debate About Style

There is considerable resistance to the "women's style of leadership theory" in the press, the executive suite, and the offices of bishops and other church leaders. At the same time that it has prompted widespread affirmation from women, it has also been the target of vociferous protest from both men and women who have found recognizing the differences in leadership style either threatening or dangerous.[32]

To reconsider whether women have a unique style, we must remember where women are right now. In the last chapter, women told us. They are searching for the attributes of their own style and *naming*. This requires claiming their own power, a psychic task that women approach with considerable ambivalence. Their own ambivalance about power causes women to have a harder time claiming their own way and naming their style effectively. Nevertheless, they are forging ahead courageously. Furthermore, they are naming their own style at the same time that they are still trying to learn how to work in the male paradigm. Finally, for the time being, it may be that they are limited to one style that is different from men's but at least acceptable to men too.

The first challenge for women, as they search for and articulate their own style or styles of leadership, is that the white male system is still the norm in management and church leadership circles. Out of survival instinct, "women frequently go along with the expectations of the white male system in order to win acceptance" either by being "proper" women or by trying to be "like men." The latter choice is common among professional women, who "believe that the only road to success is to act like men and beat them at their own game."[33]

It doesn't help that management and organizational theory tends to legitimate rather than challenge sexist practices in the workplace.[34] Sociologist Deborah Sheppard puts it this way: "Under the tremendous pressure for acceptance and conformity necessary to success at work in our social world, which are heightened greatly for women in a male-dominated environment, the differences in the ways in which women and men may formulate their experiences are generally not readily apparent." But, she adds, "while women continue to demonstrate their capacity for succeeding at 'men's work' and often excelling at it, we are realizing that under the surface of achievement, women are experiencing a work reality that differs from that of men in many ways."[35]

Many studies attempt to determine whether women do indeed have a unique style.[36] Because the outcomes are inconclusive or tend to show that women and men in church leadership have more in common than they have in difference, some researchers are concluding that women do not have a unique style. I would predict that any study of women's leadership style would be inconclusive at best, because it is not possible to study women outside patriarchy. We simply cannot know how women would lead without the constraints of the prevailing paradigm affecting them.

There is great danger for women in articulating differences. If the woman's own paradigm for leadership has not been accepted, she will be judged "weak" by the white male paradigm.[37] For this reason, some assert that clarifying differences is risky.[38] Someone will surely use them to justify unequal treatment of women. Indeed, the prejudice that difference is weakness comes from our tendency to dualistic thinking and remains the primary barrier to women and minorities in the workplace.[39] This should not be, says Sheppard, who debunks the argument that affirming differences should jeopardize equality. It's an "implicit assumption," she says, that "evidence of a difference is ideological and discriminatory." Rosener herself never said that women's leadership is better than men's. Just different.[40]

Unfortunately, it doesn't help much to assert that there is no difference between women and men in leadership. Women who demonstrate masculine traits in their leadership style can't win either. Schaef warns that women who "are too successful" by white male system standards are punished. In 1994 this theme was played over and over by Hollywood. Most of the movie villains in that year were career women.[41] Women are admonished for being "too assertive, direct, goal oriented, visible, or powerful." It happens to women working in the church as well as the corporation.[42] This, of course, is exactly what happened to our hapless manager who was seeking a promotion. The board had nearly denied her the promotion, in part because she was "too assertive." It was not because she was ineffective. In fact, a man in her position, behaving the way she did, would have been affirmed. She was evaluated, and found wanting because she did such a good job of adopting a masculine style of assertiveness in her work. But she was a woman, and wasn't supposed to be so assertive! Had she been less assertive and possibly accomplished less, she would have been judged ineffective in her job. Furthermore, even though her supervisor did see that his female manager was being judged unfairly by a white male paradigm, he accepted the paradigm as a "given."

And what of our would-be ordained campus pastor? She was "uppity" in asking for ordination rather than being content to continue her ministry as a laywoman, a status that would obviously have made the men in her denomination more comfortable. She had genuine intent. It was, she said, "a logical step in my calling, ministry and vocational journey. I [felt] God's leadership in it." And that was exactly the problem, said the deacons. She had the audacity to ask to be ordained as one of God's leaders.

These women are hard-pressed to remember that they are not the problem. The problem is systems that cannot embrace their paradigm for leadership. Thus to the architect of any quota system, I would say that it is not enough to bring women into leadership. In fact, it is a violence against women that they are brought in and then "set up" by an alien system. On the one hand, they are expected to stop being "like women." On the other hand, when they do try to "act like a man would," they are judged harshly. "The biggest obstacle women face is the most intangible. Men at the top feel uncomfortable with women around them."[43]

The Numbers Don't Lie

Though it is widely believed that women lack staying power in senior management ranks because they have overriding childcare or other family concerns, research is revealing a different problem. Women are no more likely than men to cite concerns about family or children as reasons for leaving. Nor do they leave over excessive job stress. Women leave management posts, in some cases "giving up" on their careers entirely, because they have less advancement opportunity.[44] They hit what is popularly called "the glass ceiling." A more appropriate metaphor may be a cross sectional geological diagram, says Felice Schwartz. "The barriers to women's leadership occur when potentially counterproductive layers of influence on women—maternity, tradition, socialization—meet management strata pervaded by the largely unconscious preconceptions, stereotypes, and expectations of men. Such interfaces do not exist for men, and tend to be impermeable for women."[45] They may be even more impermeable for black women, who do not enjoy an advantage in the workplace because of their race and gender. Murrell's study of U.S. Census figures and other data shows that black women don't get a boost from company policies favoring minorities and females. "Sexuality is an issue for all women, but it's harder for black women to debunk the mythology about who they are."[46] Schwartz concludes: "The most critical barrier for women of any race is the white male system's inability to recognize and value a woman's paradigm for leadership."

The stated reason for not advancing a woman might be that "She wouldn't want this overseas assignment," or "She doesn't have the right kind of experience for this promotion," or "Her family concerns will not allow her to devote her time to this assignment," or "She's not tough enough for this." Underlying all of these reasons is the real reason: "We (men) are uncomfortable (or unfamiliar) with her style." Men will make this mistake often without malicious intent, because they do not even recognize the woman's paradigm of leadership.[47]

Statistics show that in traditional organizations, it is very difficult for new paradigms (outside the accepted white male norm) to be recognized and valued. Nearly thirty years after Betty Friedan called upon women to join men in the world of work, only 3 percent of top executive jobs in the largest companies in the U.S. are held by women.

The wage gap between women and men is 25 to 35 percent for administrative, managerial, and executive positions. Furthermore, more women than men report that they are unlikely to remain in their present jobs, and that they are looking for jobs that will provide them with more career opportunity.[48]

The numbers warn us that women are still having difficulty breaking into leadership in the church as well. Though the ordination of women is not new in most Protestant denominations, a study conducted by the National Council of Churches in 1988 put women at only 7.9 percent of the ordained clergy among denominations ordaining women in North America. This percentage was an increase of 4 percent during the period 1978 to 1988. More recent figures show that, in all but a few denominations, the percentage of clergy who are women has decreased, even though there has been a dramatic rise in the absolute numbers of women entering the profession.[49]

In recent years, the number of women attending theological schools has also risen sharply. It is yet unclear whether women will have an easier time entering the clergy pool and moving within the system as their numbers increase.[50] Clergywomen continue to report frequent difficulty obtaining a first call, and patterns of lay resistance documented in 1981 persist. Once in the system, clergywomen's ability to move up is hampered and they continue to be called to smaller, less secure congregations in some denominations. This fact, of course, affects their level of compensation as well. Once in the parish there is growing evidence that clergywomen are accepted by parishioners; nevertheless, very recent studies confirm the particular difficulty clergywomen have in moving into senior pastorates.[51] Thus "even when the way to ordination is open, women often find themselves in but still out."[52]

Outside the ordained clergy, many thousands of women work in church leadership in professional positions and as volunteers. Records are not kept of these women in the same way that records are kept of clergy.[53] Research shedding light on how well they are accepted, how long they stay, what their leadership is like and other factors that would indicate their success is not being conducted either.[54]

The modest qualitative findings of this project represent some of the first research done among a broad spectrum of Protestant women: clergy, lay professionals, and volunteers. Thus, it is difficult to present any picture of how women are faring from a research or statistical point of view. Perhaps the absence of information says enough in itself about how women are doing. Anecdotal reports by women in specific denominations, on the other hand, are available from women themselves. These reports tell a story not much different than what the statistics tell us about women in the clergy ranks: women at all levels of church work struggle to be seen and heard, indeed, to have a place.[55]

— — Chapter Four — —

The Church as an Environment for Women

Yes, I think the climate here is generally quite receptive to women in leadership—at least I thought so when I came here."

This was often the first response when I asked women how welcome they have felt in the church. Women who aspire to leadership look to the church with great hope. For one thing, they know that they have much to contribute. For another, they see the church as having great possibility as a friendly work environment for women. The church may rightly be judged a good candidate for success in embracing the more collaborative styles of leadership that women exhibit. The Christian faith itself is based on the feminine principle of paradox.[1] Furthermore, within congregations and church management circles there seems to be a higher level of comfort with the idea of partnership rather than hierarchy, and a significant number of men who themselves use a collaborative leadership style.[2]

A recent study of male-female church staffs points out that "Clergymen are not necessarily representative of men in our culture: some clergymen do want power in order to influence and persuade, but other clergymen want power in order to help empower others."[3] These authors cite one study in which more than 50 percent of male and 80 percent of female clergy "preferred having power in order to have and share resources with others."[4] Furthermore, they add, "men and women in ministry tend toward psychological androgyny; that is, they experience the integration of both masculine and feminine qualities."[5]

This kind of healthy blending of the masculine and feminine is expected in the church. It's part of the stereotype. As one clergywoman puts it: "If there's going to be one organization in society that can accommodate the human realities, it should be the church." The church at its best, a clergyman agrees, "is a group of people with a common mind and common purpose, who care about each other." Unfortunately, he adds, "the institutions of the church can be mean, nasty, and uncaring. I have seen them crush people. Sometimes in the institution of the church we lose the strength of the local church, the nurturing, caring community. We find ourselves getting into issues of power and competition." Another clergyman sees the frailty of the church as inevitable, as with any other ogranization: "I thought it was going to be different working for the church, sure. But why should it be? We try to be a caring community, but we still are an organization with a job to do."

Women and men who are called to the work of the church share these wishes, that work in the church will be more participatory, person-centered, and network-based rather than power-based. They would all like leadership to embrace more collaborative paradigms. Unfortunately, says one clergyman philosophically, "The church has lots of good instincts, many of which are in conflict with each other. It does seem that the church has become an advocate for a more ethical and compassionate stance (toward women), and for equality, but it has not come to terms adequately with the sin that it embodies in itself."

Unfortunately, the "people" who are crushed by the church are often women. One clergywoman puts it bluntly: "In some ways it's worse here. There is this myth of the partnership of men and women in the church, and that myth hides a lot of ambivalence and a lot of disparity."

The fact is, women in leadership get a mixed message from the church. On the one hand, they are welcome. On the other hand, they are not. On the one hand, they are verbally and structurally welcomed, by pronouncements of the church stating the intention to have grow-ing numbers of women in leadership, by quotas that make sure they are there, by invitations to speak and in other ways be visible, by celebrations of the Decade in Solidarity with them, by men who defy the displeasure of their powerful brothers to advocate with them for the ordination of women in more and more Protestant denominations, and by many other individual and denominational actions. On the other hand, they are made unwelcome, either explicitly or implicitly, by habits of language that exclude them, by an entrenched male hierarchy in the clergy ranks, by male theological dogma and thinking, and by an enduring fear of their sexuality that is the legacy of a patriarchal Christianity. What we are experiencing, says one clergy-woman, "is the creaking of an ancient heavy door, slowly opening, with some pulling it open and others pushing it closed."[6]

The Church Hierarchy and Its Response to Women

The numbers and the anecdotal reports of women[7] should cause us to suspect that the denominations are still typical of exclusive organizations, having both practices that tell women they are not full members, and, even where inclusion is intended, maintaining cultural barriers that are embedded within the organization.[8] It is these organizational and cultural barriers that cause women of faith to experience "cognitive dissonance, a contradiction between ideas and actual experience," when they turn from reading the Gospels to looking at the way the gospel message has been interpreted by the church for many centuries.[9]

THEME THREE: Women get a mixed message from the church.

Though the church does embrace collaborative leadership better than many institutions, and certainly a great deal better than the business world, it does so within a system that is in other ways religiously hierarchical and theologically grounded in the prevailing white male system of thinking.[10] In order to remain thus grounded, the church actually casts off the feminine principles that are at the heart of the faith, devalues experience as a grounding for theology or practice, and hotly debates the value of diversity in its ranks. This does not happen because the people of the church want it so, or because any of us is cavalier about the fundamental values of the faith. It happens because the prevailing system of our culture has no theology of differences.[11] The result is that men and women working together in the church get caught trying to be collaborative in systems that are hierarchical.[12]

Jackson Carroll provides a good summary of how the church came to be a male-dominated hierarchy, how the influences of the Middle

Ages entrenched hierarchy, and how feminist theologians today rightly call for a return to more symmetrical, interdependent relationships that are, contrary to what we might think, more in line with Paul's vision of the church.[13] We are advised to remember that "at our tradition's heart is not a patriarchal encounter between the sexes but an assertion that 'from the beginning of creation God made them male and female' (Mark 10:6, cf. Gen. 1:27); that the dominance of male over female is a mark not of humanity as created and intended by God but of humanity disobedient and rebellious (Gen. 3:16); and following from this (as Paul observes) that among the baptized there can in the matter of status be 'neither Jew nor Greek, neither bond nor free, neither male nor female' but only 'all one in Christ Jesus' (Gal. 3:28)."[14] Letty Russell's image for this is "church in the round" and she asserts that to achieve the egalitarian vision, we will have to "overturn the master's tables and challenge the tradition of the patriarchal household."[15]

The most obvious way in which the male hierarchy entangles women and hinders their leadership is in its endless debates about ordination.[16] Carroll, Hargrove, and Lummis, authors of a well-regarded study of women in ministry at Hartford Seminary in the early 1980s, provide helpful background to the ordination debates by pointing out when and why women are allowed to have any leadership role in a religious movement (when it is young and when it is mature, but less when it is in the "consolidation and organization phase, when women are absorbed into a system dominated by men and are not allowed much autonomy of expression"), the role of societal trends in aiding women's growing role in the denominations, and the factors that cause women to seek ordination in the first place.[17]

Many denominations now ordain women,[18] but it's not so clear what that means.[19] In chapter 3 we reviewed how lay and clergy women are faring in getting jobs. Some of the reasons that women struggle provide insight into the hierarchy itself. The Episcopal Church's option whereby bishops can choose to ordain or not ordain women is a widely known loophole for the hierarchy. Not so well known is the "visiting bishop" policy, whereby a parish can invite a bishop from outside its own diocese to perform the rites of the church.[20] This loophole for local sovereignty establishes the kind of congregationalism that allows parishes the option not to work with their own bishop, for whatever reason. The motive seems transparent, since the policy came into being just as the church consecrated Barbara Harris as its first female bishop in 1989.

In other denominations, women continue to be frustrated about bishops or other male officials who politically support their right to be clergy, but do nothing structurally to make sure that they get jobs. "The law doesn't necessarily change attitudes," as one clergywoman points out. And surely it is true that attitudes in the individual congregation govern, in the end, whether a woman is called to ministry there. But what do the hierarchies do to institute teaching that will help congregational attitudes grow into an acceptance of women? "It is my bishop's job to let congregations know they can't reject women candidates just because they are women," stresses one clergywoman. "He needs to be very objective when this happens." Unfortunately, not all bishops are willing to fight this battle.

So much of this goes on (or doesn't go on) in the hierarchies of mainline denominations that women in more conservative churches, which do not allow their ordination, wonder aloud whether their ordained sisters are much better off. Here is an irony. For on this point, the most conservative and most liberal of women agree with one another about the uselessness of ordination—for radically different reasons. Just as there are conservative women who question the advantage of ordination, there are other women who consider ordination in a male-established and still male-dominated hierarchy "at best meaningless and at worst betrayal."[21] Useful or not, ordination is women's ticket to the ranks of power, and refusal to ordain remains "a patent act of exclusion" and "a potent symbol of other, less easily described exclusions."[22]

Once women clergy are placed in jobs in congregations, the hierarchy does not help them much more. Clergywomen must now win over their male colleagues or, more often, negotiate the maze of traps we'll discuss in part 2 of this book. They're pretty much on their own in doing it. The Reverend Donna Schaper has created a hilarious metaphor, a story about her lawnmower to explain what it's like to be a woman in ministry in the church today. She concludes with, "whether the matter is mowing my lawn or practicing my profession, men seem to be everywhere. I wonder if they feel our presence as acutely. My mind is always full of male voices. Commenting inarticulately. Telling me how to do it better."[23]

A Hierarchy Hard-of-Hearing

The hierarchy also shows its true colors in the way it reacts to women's voices. Make no mistake. "The question of women is a powerful symbol . . . for many of the issues that trouble the church in the United States and the world today. These issues range from the most intimate, private questions of sexuality and family to the most public: questions of institutional authority, democratic process, equality of rights and responsibilities, dissent, the nature of the common good and of justice itself in the Christian context."[24] And it is a gauge of the seriousness of the issues that women are so often and so brutally cut down by the hierarchy when they try to raise their voices.

Two very visible incidents come to mind. The first was in Canberra, Australia, at the 1991 World Council of Churches Assembly. Two presenters from different traditions were asked to comment on the meaning of the theme "Come Holy Spirit, renew the whole creation." The absent Patriarch Parthenios of Egypt had a paper read to the assembly by an Orthodox theologian. By contrast, Professor Chung Hyun Kyung used the ancient rituals of her native Korea to express the Spirit's presence. The reaction, especially from some of the more conservative churches present, was condemnation and questioning. What was she doing? Was she trivializing theology? Was this syncretism? The controversy Kyung evoked "was most certainly in part a controversy over whom theology will serve and whether or not the Lord has spoken only through white Western male theologians."[25]

The same could be said about controversy surrounding the 1993 conference "Re-Imagining . . . God, the Community, the Church," an event of the Ecumenical Decade in Solidarity with Women. The conference, which "sought to incorporate women's lives and experiences into metaphors of God that traditionally have been expressed differently . . . to blend traditional imagery about God with some new images,"[26] drew charges of paganism, among other things, from a number of denominations whose women participated.[27] Regardless of what we might think of the content of the conference, it should be a reminder to us that women will confront patriarchal authority with their own voices and images.[28] Nonetheless, women are scarred by the burning criticism. The conference and its stormy aftermath in the denominations has led church women to a rueful answer to the question: Can we image God? "Apparently not. Look what happened to us when we tried!"

A final look at the institutional churches and their relationships to women focuses on hierarchical response to "women's issues"—domestic violence, child care, harassment, wages, women's poverty, and the like. The fact that these are still so often named as only women's issues is telling in itself, but my point goes beyond this observation. Because bureaucracies are still controlled by men and governed by the rules of the white male system, the response of the denominations on these issues often misses the mark badly. Kathy's story provides a good example.[29]

As pastor in a large congregation, Kathy discovered that she had been the victim of long-forgotten abuse in her childhood. She sought professional guidance. In the course of working out her memories, she experienced the rage that is so well known to be a part of the healing process. Kathy went to her bishop to share basic information about her struggle. She did not wish to do so but realized it was necessary. Should she seem "different" to her colleagues at the church, she wanted someone, confidentially, to know why. Some months later, well into Kathy's process of healing, she was fired without the bishop raising a hand to help her "because others here say you are too angry, and they cannot work with you." This was the first time Kathy had heard of any concerns at work, and this incident represented the only way in which Kathy's personal situation was ever addressed or commented on by her bishop. This happened in a denomination that has officially stated its support of women recovering from abuse.

As shocking as this story is, the lesson behind it is not that women are mistreated by the church for disclosing their vulnerable pain. Men lose their jobs too when disclosing that they are depressed or angry. The lesson is much more subtle, and it cuts to the fatal flaw of a hierarchy that is founded on the survival of the fittest. A hierarchy will make a statement, have a pronouncement, or do something official to address a social wrong. The trouble with this kind of response is that the pronouncement never resolves anything unless it is backed up by leaders who know the heart and soul of the problem itself. In the case of sexual or physical abuse, which most of the denominations are quick to comment about these days, no official position, no statement, no word of any kind makes any difference at all unless the people at the top take the trouble to know the problem and its victims in a personal way. Once Kathy's church had an official position on abuse, the very existence of that statement should have been a mandate for every supervisor—female and male—to find out about the healing process intimately enough that he or she could work with recovering victims to keep the workplace and the individual safe. That's the very point of having a statement. And in the church, because the hierarchy is so male dominated at the top, men carry a heavy responsibility to know about these "women's issues" in very personal ways. Unfortunately, hierarchies seldom work this way. Certainly, the hierarchy of the church does not. Because of the very nature of patriarchal hierarchy, men don't get the assistance they need to know what they need to know about women. What happens, then, is that many Kathys receive negative communication about themselves, their ability and their self-worth from a hierarchy that cannot be responsive to their life issues.

Being the Elect

Our discussion of the hierarchy illustrates the flaw of any dominant group. It forgets that others are not like them. And so, the dominant group—in our case the white male European hierarchy of the church—is caught in a dilemma. It ends up trying "to build community by eliminating diversity: by excluding the 'others' or by welcoming them to become like 'us.' " The hierarchy, by its very nature, cannot achieve diversity. The result is that women and minorities have been taught by the patriarchy "that community means sameness, uniformity, control."[30] That's why the church cannot hear women very well, cannot help them succeed in the system, cannot embrace their images without fear, cannot, in the end, know the unknown Other who is a woman.

Thus, one clergywoman has this to say after seven years of service in her denomination: "No one is really asking my opinion. I thought when they made this big deal about having a certain percentage of women here, they had some expectation about what that was going to mean—that there would be an intention to include women in decision-making circles. But that has never, never happened."

Another clergywoman put it more bluntly: "I finally figured out that I'm not supposed to change anything here. I'm just supposed to work here."

United Methodist Diaconal Minister Rena Yocum calls this "ungifting." Women, she says, "have time and time again had the painful experience of the church ungifting our gifts. Our gifts are deemed undesirable because they do not match the ecclesial furniture or because they are not like anything anybody has envisioned." Ungifting, she adds, "is a denial, a denial of the giver as well as the gifts."[31] It is, of course, not only women and minorities who are excluded. The nature of the patriarchal paradigm "represents a socio-cultural system in which a few men have power over other men, women, children, slaves, and colonialized people."[32] Thus men can be victims of hierarchy too. One woman, upon her appointment to a denominational post, actually drew a pyramid to show all the things that had to happen in a hierarchical system for her to "be elected." It's a graphic illustration of the nature of hierarchy.

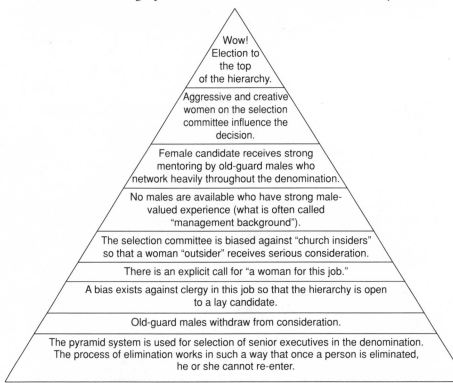

Selection in the hierarchy works from the bottom up and forms a pyramid.

It seems impossible for women to change the church power structures by bringing new views of power, leadership, and decision making into the ranks. It is not enough to "be there" so long as the prevailing system is hierarchical by nature. It will take more than the "joining with men in leadership" to "create new leadership styles that combine feminine and masculine gifts."[33] What is required as well is a change in the prevailing paradigm, a fundamental change in the nature of authority such that it is not based on hierarchy.[34]

This is radical. It is also biblical. "Election provides a source of identity in a particular socio-historical reality," as it did for the Israelites. "But it becomes contradictory when abstracted as a doctrine applicable to all realities. Without grounding in a reality of oppression, election quickly moves from a gift of grace to a justification of privilege." This is exactly what has happened in the formation of the church hierarchy. "A source of identity in the formation of a struggling community of faithful people quickly became deformed by a hierarchy of orthodoxy and exclusion by those who became the dominant political and religious leaders in Protestant areas of Europe and North America." When we have combined "the idea that election is a free gift of God's grace with the idea that election is a form of privilege that justifies the domination and exclusion of others,"[35] we have distorted the doctrine of election.

The hierarchy of the church does not represent the elect. Privilege is not the purpose of election. Identity is, but it is surely not the church hierarchy that needs a source of greater identity. When the hierarchy forgets that its purpose is to be changed as much as it changes others, it has lost its prophetic stance. By its very nature it cannot be welcoming of women.

The Evangelical Environment

Whenever we talk about a hierarchy that is hard-of-hearing, we must acknowledge that, within the fundamentalist streams among evangelical systems,[36] there are denominations that do not want to hear women at all. They have tried, with rhetoric more than practice, to silence women completely.[37] How this view became entrenched, and how women now respond to it, is worthy of some note before we leave the subject of the church as hierarchy and its relationship to women.

Fundamentalists and Pentecostals were not always so restricting of their women. In fact, in the nineteenth century, and as the women's suffrage movement finally succeeded by 1920, women were allowed quite expansive roles.[38] For a variety of reasons documented by others,[39] fundamentalist males and Pentecostal hierarchies are now much more restricting of women in leadership. The exact time and nature of that change is a point of debate in fundamentalism.[40] One view is that "while trends in other Protestant organizations inched toward greater equality for women (in the decade after World War I), rising fundamentalist organizations segregated or excluded them."[41]

The other view: women continued to have considerable opportunity for ministry, though typically those opportunities were outside the ordained ministry. Because evangelical Protestants are more likely to be a "neo-ecclesiastical, market-driven popular religious movement" that is built on a "foundation of independent, entrepreneurial, special purpose organizations," it has in some ways been easier (than in mainline denominations) for women to gain entry at most levels. Because by definition fundamentalists were disestablished from the mainstream culture, "Authority in fundamentalism tended to work from the grass roots upward," rather than downward, through a male-dominated hierarchy, as is typical of the mainline denominations. In addition, there were many ministry roles available in fundamentalism, where women staffed a massive missionary movement, taught Christian education, became Bible translators and the like, while women in the mainline denominations fought a losing battle with the hierarchy for appointments in declining churches in a thoroughly male-dominated system.[42] Both history and an overabundance of strident rhetoric against the leadership of women, which does not seem to have any relationship to real practice, have obscured reality so that a return to original sources to uncover the real role of women is often necessary.

The debate turns on rhetoric. Since the neoevangelical and Pentecostal denominations are not hierarchies like the mainline denominations, it is not hierarchy that controls women. It is rhetoric. The theme song of fundamentalist rhetoric puts women under the authority of men, and restricts them to the home sphere, or at best the foreign missionary sphere where they are "out of sight." Even for those who have chosen such ministries, it takes only a few short years for the rhetoric to silence them altogether. The background music of the culture between the World Wars was very harmonious to this stance: women were encouraged to the profession of wife and mother. But today, the background music is quite different, and not at all harmonious. Women are encouraged to take on public roles, to work outside the home. And now, even in the neoevangelical and Pentecostal denominations, more women seek ordination, pastoral calls, and a public role that is visible.

Though some neoevangelical and Pentecostal denominations ordain women,[43] the actual ordination usually depends on the will of the congregation or the district superintendent. Women do not often fare very well in finding a congregation to ordain them or in seeking jobs when the superintendent must acknowledge the fruit of their vocation. Statistics show that in several denominations in the neoevangelical spectrum, the number of ordained women is decreasing sharply.[44] In the Southern Baptist Church, though the number of ordained women is increasing, the number pastoring congregations has decreased sharply since the denomination took a turn toward fundamentalism in the late 1970s. In 1984, the Southern Baptist Convention took a stand against the ordination of women and local Baptist Associations regularly "disfellowship" congregations that ignore the ban. Predictions are that "even with good intentions and efforts by some, it is clear that no dramatic change can be expected toward the universal acceptance of clergywomen among Southern Baptists . . . particularly . . . as long as the overall theological and political climate is dominated by fundamentalists."[45]

Within fundamentalism, with its narrow view of woman's capability, women must function differently. They play at least three different roles. First, some women agree with the rhetoric that silences them, accepting as proper the authority of their husbands over them and the limited public voice that they are allowed. These are the Traditionals. One woman puts it this way: "God said women should remain silent in the church, and yes, he said it in that culture, but we believe it applies to all cultures. I am very comfortable with that."

Within these boundaries, women can still function effectively as leaders, though they often anger other women who see them as selling out. They are accepted by men and even encouraged in their leadership. One woman in this situation characterized her denomination as "the church that has the strictest approach to the role of women, and at the same time is the most open to women in leadership." Another woman who has since left her conservative denomination for a mainline ministry had a different view: "As long as I knew what my place was and I stayed within those boundaries, there was room. There was opportunity for leadership." Sociologists confirm that a woman in a restrictive setting will not be marginalized unless she decides "to rise above her marginality and aspires to become an active participant in an institutional position that heretofore had not been open to women. Then fireworks begin."[46]

A second role that women play in this situation is that of Catalyst. These are women who, much like the Traditionals, function inside a male-dominant setting without objecting openly to the restrictions placed upon them, but silently working to demonstrate the capability of women. One woman puts it this way: "I really just want to serve the Lord in whichever way I can, with whatever gifts and talents he gave me, and I'm not trying to prove any point. But I will stand up for women and their gifts and their ability and all of the things that go with that." These are real risk takers, agents inside an enemy camp. But the secret of their success is that they do not view their denomination or the men around them as enemies. They don't even necessarily see themselves as having a hidden agenda. They just know that change is coming to their denomination and they have been called to help prepare the way. They typically agree that change is necessary and biblical, though they take care not to say so. Their role is to prepare men in their denomination for the inevitable changes that will allow women full range of leadership in the church, including ordination. And finally, they will never say so to anyone who would jeopardize their role.

A third type of woman is most well known. She is the Reformer. She takes the most active role in bringing about change for the leadership of women. It is with her that "the fireworks begin." The first wave of Reformers have to be outspoken and tough to hold their ground. Later, as gains are made, they can be softer, stronger, team players, though the idea that they should be is in itself a culturally imposed value. Contrary to their public image, Reformers do not necessarily have an agenda either. They just want to do what they are called to do, and it happens that they are called to a vocation forbidden to women. Baptist minister Raye Nell Dyer is a case in point. Her situation was outlined briefly in the opening of chapter 3. After nine years of successful campus ministry as an unordained woman, she asked for ordination and was caught in a maelstrom of controversy in the Texas Baptist Association. Raye is a Reformer because she asked for something forbidden. Texas Baptist Association officials say ordination is a secondary issue in the dispute. The real problem "is that she pushed for it."[47]

We have not yet reached a point of integrating women into leadership in the church so that we even have a fourth kind of woman, the woman who can just be herself without carrying any extra burden on behalf of herself and her sisters. Another option, of course, is for women to leave the producers of fundamentalist rhetoric in search of leadership roles in the mainline churches. Some women do this. In fact, the dramatic drop in the numbers of female clergy in some conservative denominations leads to speculation that they are beginning to do so in large numbers.

But other women stay. Why? Women all over the Christian landscape ask themselves and each other this question often. The WomenChurch movement offers an option to patriarchal Christianity, and there are other options as well, here and around the globe.[48] Why stay, particularly in a denomination that denies women a voice as well as a leadership role?[49] Women stay for relationships, or for the option of a more personal emotive faith experience that they believe the evangelical tradition promotes. They stay because, sometimes, they don't know leaving is an option, or because they think the problem is them and not the church, or because they believe the Bible tells them to be submissive. They stay to be an example, to contribute, to help younger women, to bring about change. They stay because they don't believe their sisters in the mainline denominations are much better off. They stay because they are called to stay. But most of all they stay because they love their church. Says Rita Nakashima Brock of her church: "I refuse to surrender it to those who want me out of it."[50]

— — Chapter Five — —

The Sexuality of Denominations

A laywoman who has served widely in ecumenical circles for many years has said: "To gain respect you have to stick around long enough, and of course, a lot of women are rejected out of hand in church circles, especially global circles, where there are very few of us. But if you stick around long enough, and if you are tough enough, and if you are nice enough, *and most of all if when they look at you they don't think about sex, it will be all right.*"

She makes a point that is obvious to all women, but is nevertheless, deeply troubling: the very presence of women in the church is unsettling to the psychic imagination of men. In an ardently masculine sexual environment, women stand out as the unknown Other, a source of fear and temptation.

This posture toward women is also revealed by the comment overheard by a woman priest: "Who was that hussy behind the altar?"[1]

The strands of historical and cultural development that have resulted in the fear and hatred of women are varied and complex, but now so intertwined with our way of viewing our moral universe that we can hardly separate them anymore. They are at the heart of what we might call the sexuality of the denominations.

The Sexuality of Denominations

A critical environmental concern for women working in the church is this sexuality of the denominations.[2] Admittedly, sexuality is a difficult thing to define, and its interplay with gender is complex and variously interpreted by sociologists, psychiatrists, and theologians.

Both sexuality and gender are largely ignored as concepts of any concern to the workplace. They are nevertheless deeply imbedded in the nature of the denominations as organizations, as we shall see in this chapter.

It is obvious to even the most casual viewer that the denominations—mainline and evangelical—are deeply antifeminine and fundamentally masculine in their sexual orientation. All denominations to some degree (except perhaps the Quakers and the ascetic Shakers) still rely on biological essentialism to assert the supremacy of the male gender. They assert that it is in the nature of man—*in his sexuality*—that he is superior to woman. What sociologists call biological essentialism, feminist theologians call the doctrine of fixed natures, which dictates a prescribed destiny for women based on their biology. It's an idea still widely accepted "because its stereotypes are older and deeper in our culture than any others."[3] It is precisely this argument that has been used for centuries to keep women out of the priesthood or pastorate and, as we shall see, still underlies our understanding of the church and the way in which we construct our faith, in a most fundamental way.

Out of this framework grows the habit of sexual zoning, a sociological term that describes how organizations create a geography of access to certain types of experiences for one sex only. In the denominations, it is significant that certain types of religious leadership experiences are still largely reserved for men because of men's physical nature, which supposedly makes them more like Christ. A simple example is preaching, which is "territory open only to the male pastor" in denominations that do not ordain women. Even in denominations that do ordain women, it's territory seldom open to them, by virtue of the fact that so few ever become solo or senior pastors.

The predominantly male sexuality in denominations is constructed in a larger environment of sexual negativity. In the Judeo-Christian tradition, the historical weight of religious, intellectual, and moral opinion has accumulated against sexuality. We consider sexuality frightening, uncontrollable, illegitimate, chaotic, unpredictable, even bad. It is something we strive mightily to limit, control, and keep private.[4] Men are victimized in a unique way by this view, living as they do as preeminent embodiments of the favored sex in an environment that would rather we all be without sex, if that were possible. They are forced to suppress their sexuality, and we now see the dark side of this sexuality emerging in an overwhelming abundance of cases of clergy sexual misconduct. But women have much more to overcome as individual persons living and working in an environment sexualized to be masculine. We shall examine just how much they are affected by a deeper look into the sexuality of denominations and its resulting theology and language.

Some definitions and clarifications are in order. First, in our every-day discourse, we often confuse gender and sexuality. Gender is the sex we are, and we are each still one or the other. Sexuality is our quality of being sexual, and this takes many forms. Intertwined as they are, sexuality and gender are different. Furthermore, it's not only people who are sexual. Sexuality can be attributed to organizations just as it is assigned to individuals. It is therefore not just a distinct feature of our private lives or our private selves, but also "an ordinary and frequent public process." In applying the notion of sexuality to the denomina-tions, I do not mean to imply that sexuality can be organized. In fact it is diverse and diffuse, defying organization.[5]

It may still seem odd somehow to think of the denominations from a sexual point of view. While sexuality may be "the most obvious element of gender relations in terms of common sense, phenomenology, and everyday gossip, it has remained the most unexamined within organiza-tional theory."[6] It is not a popular topic for academic analysis, subject as it is to sarcasm, hostility, and censorship. The only way in which we do see and examine our sexuality as organizations is within the context of the new sexual debates about human sexuality, including (for example) abor-tion and gay and lesbian liberation. These debates, though vastly different in most aspects, have in common the tendency to make the expression of our sexuality into a problem. Many denominations have fallen victim to the no-win traps of examining their sexuality in relation to these specific questions only. In examining the sexuality of denominations more thor-oughly, I do not wish to titillate or embarrass, but to cast a brighter light on the whole of the matter and therein to examine the effect on women in leadership in the church.

Sexuality, Eve, and That Serpent

In a patriarchy, woman is always the Other, the antithesis over against which one defines authentic (male) selfhood.[7] The patriarchal paradigm defines the sexuality of our denominations as male. As early as the first century, male philosophy aligned the masculine with transcendence, the spiritual, and the intellect, and women with nature and the physical. Our tendency to dualistic thinking added that male was better; female inferior. The Aristotelian dishing up of this concoction goes something like this: women are biologically defective males, merely the vessels that hold the potency of men. They symbolize the passivity and inferiority of nature.[8]

Several centuries later, Augustine put it theologically, attaching the inferiority of women to the creation stories. His view went beyond the simple woman-is-inferior theme, adding that God *intended* her inferiority. We know this, he said, because Eve's creation was dependent on Adam.[9] It was a short leap from that view to the Christian concept of woman "made only for procreation; a helpmeet for man in the only area where he cannot be served better by a male."[10] Our early church fathers found it easy to agree about assigning women secondary biological status, but they had an argument about her soul. Augustine did not believe that woman's soul was as inferior as her body. Others did. And of course what any woman thought about this was of no account.

The theology went like this: Eve bore the primary responsibility for the fall of humankind all by herself. Her actions relegate her soul to secondary status, and require the abasement of all women and the covering of their shameful female nature for all time. After Augustine thought about the creation stories a bit longer—and decided that spontaneous sexual desire was the proof of and penalty for original sin—the indictment was complete. (The next step was celibacy for priests who needed to perish thoughts about an evil temptress.) Woman was also blamed for the existence of evil. It was in the nature of woman—*in her sexuality*—to be evil. Connected as women were with the physical and the sexual, it seemed natural, rational (and no doubt comforting) to blame them for the *de facto* existence of evil in the world. The argument worked so well that Eve is almost more maligned than the serpent-devil. It was very clever. Our venerable church fathers, the architects of Christian patriarchy, achieved both a theological explanation and a practical justification for male dominance and female subservience.[11]

In actual fact, the status to which women were assigned so many centuries ago by male philosophers and theologians has more to do with men than it does with women. It has to do with man's fear of woman, his inability to control his libido, and his need to place responsibility for it somewhere else. Augustine himself was known to be puzzled, revolted, and possibly also frightened by the power of his own sexual drive.[12] It gave women tremendous power, a power that could be neutralized by the labels "inferior" and "evil." Even more likely, Augustine's theology about women was a way of dealing with his own—and therefore man's—essential nature. Nevertheless, other church fathers take up the cause against women and the theme is repeated in the literature, theology, and language of the church. Christian women have been consigned to an inferior status ever since.[13]

By now we have forgotten that Augustine's sexual interpretation of the creation stories would have astounded the Christians of the first century and their Jewish and pagan contemporaries.[14] In fact, the early Christians interpreted the story of Adam and Eve as having little or nothing to do with sexuality or carnal knowledge, a historical fact that may be surprising to us. To the extent that it is, it indicates how we have been captivated by the moral implications of Augustine's view of the creation stories, even though we may not read the stories themselves literally.

In the centuries since Augustine, the church has developed elaborate theological systems that remind women of their supposed innate inferiority, based on the biological fact that they are closely tied to the physical and somehow responsible for evil in the world. This posture of discomfort that the Christian tradition shows to women has had profound effect on our collective unconscious. Women have become "standard-bearers" of the sexual, uncomfortable reminders that we are all sexual beings. Since the Christian tradition is still uncomfortable with the physical, and particularly the sexual, the very presence of women remains deeply troubling for the church. The fact that sexuality is a major identifying characteristic of the white male system,[15] combined with the fact that church systems and theologies are so firmly grounded in white male system thinking, exacerbates this problem. We are left, as a result, with three limited images for women: whore, wife, and virgin.[16] When these images pervade our self-conscious, how can we possibly see her as pastor or leader?

But put aside the early theologians of the church for a moment. There are other influences on the imagination that cause women to be feared. Classical mythology is full of stories of the devouring mother. These are stories of woman's power, which is considerable but smothered. It is she who gives us all life and nurtures or withholds from us when we are helpless infants.[17] And in growing up, it is the ultimate task for the male to define himself as different from her. In a patriarchy, woman's power must be suppressed and her mystery must never be known. It is in the nature of the known (male) to wonder about and fear the unknown (female).

Ancient mythic systems, though vastly different, all include this theme. The Phrygian myths of the great earth mother Cybele tell the fate of her son-lover Attis, who was castrated for secretly observing women's rites and being unfaithful to her. Isthtar, a major goddess in the Assyro-Babylonian pantheon, emasculates and slays a new son-lover every year. In Hebrew mythology, one of the Mary stories tells of a Jewess who devoured her child during the siege of Jerusalem to keep him from being captured. In Hinduism, Kali is the great mother and benefactress on her right side and the fury and ogress, devourer of her own offspring, on her left side. Almost every tradition has its mythology of the emasculating or devouring mother-lover.[18] These stories remind us that woman is indeed the unknown Other.

The truth that women know about themselves is, of course, quite different. Woman is as divine as man, privileged to share with God the reenactment of birth cycles, over and over, with every moon. The image of the feminine in God is a representation of immanence, symbolic of the value of physical power that comes from within, rather than the power over. It calls to memory all the power and even the violence of creation and birth, growing, changing, living, and dying. This is the power that is honored in the Incarnation. Our natural world demonstrates these powers to us every day, and we each carry a hidden knowledge of it in the forgotten memory of our birth. Having forgotten it, we fear its return—if not before, then surely at the moment of our death. Whatever images we carry with us of the feminine holy, they are images of connectedness, sustenance, healing, creating. They are earthly, physical, and, indeed, these feminine aspects of God do represent feminine power, the power of the dark womb. It is a power that patriarchal Christianity has not embraced.[19] Yet, woman is wise to remember that she is "not merely blind nature and life force. She has a spiritual awareness of her own which has little to do with the masculine culture in which we live."[20]

Imagine then in this context, Korean theologian Chung Hyun Kyung giving her interpretation of the Holy Spirit before an audience of the World Council of Churches, which included men and women from Christian traditions all over the world: One churchwoman privileged to observe it recalls: "Here was this wonderfully beautiful woman dancing and using her body in a very beautiful and expressive way, as she created the context for her speech. Then, when her speech was over, she did more of the dancing. It was experiential. It was bodily. She asked for audience participation. She told us we were standing on holy ground and we should take our shoes off." And, afterwards she was accused of heresy. Why? Our observer continued, "The intellectual approach is so common when we discuss theology that it's hard to accept anything else, particularly when a woman does an experiential thing, and particularly when you have to look at her body. It's too much for a lot of people, just way too much."

It's "way too much" because the church has institutionalized fear of the feminine. Historically, this discomfort is illustrated by the admonition that women should cover themselves (to protect men!), the stoning of the adulteress, the burning of "witches," and a host of other rules and behaviors, including our current theological justifications for keeping women out of leadership in the church.[21] Men still seem to need "to create theological reasons for excluding women from any active role in civil or religious society in order to preserve their own dominance or cope with their sexual drives."[22]

On the conscious, rational level, most of us, both men and women, would deny that there is any such deep-seated psychological thing going on in our denominations. In fact, we may be shocked by the very idea. Certainly we would deny that the rules of patriarchy have anything to do with our fear of the feminine. But there are too many rules of that very system, and too many restrictions on participation and behavior of women in the church that can't be explained any other way. The very fact that denominations still debate about whether women should be clergy, governing board members, or even Sunday school teachers and choir members is the most obvious example of the influence of the white male system of thinking on the participation of women in church life.[23] To women and men who have broken out of these biases, the debate does not even make sense because it is based on an arrogant assumption, full of hubris: that because Jesus is the mediator, only men can "approach God" as intermediaries for the people. This idea is pure patriarchal thinking. It denies the feminine attributes of God, and betrays the church as idolatrous.[24]

In this context, deeply suspicious as it is of woman, theology and language play pivotal roles. On the one hand, our prevailing masculine theologies and our overwhelmingly male language betray the essential masculine sexuality of the denominations. This is why women wish so fervently to create theologies out of a feminine context and to speak language that is at the very least gender neutral, and at best, is allowed sometimes to be feminine. But the paradox is that, so long as the prevailing patriarchal paradigm holds fast, neither our theology nor our language will change fundamentally. Let us take a closer look.

> *THEME FOUR: In the patriarchal environment of the denominations, theology and language work against women.*

The Theological Enterprise as Male Thought

In a masculine environment, orthodox (i.e., male) theology has worked against women. Until recently, there hasn't been much theology meaningful to women and, since women have been writing and speaking their own theology, they have been subject to increased backlash in the church.

One clergywoman recounted this response to feminist theology from her male colleague: "We men don't have any male theologies. Why do you women need feminist theology?" The clergywoman replied with a silent gesture to the bookcase behind her desk. "Pick any book on the shelf," she said. To his credit, her male colleague assented with a silent "aha!" What he didn't realize until it was pointed out to him is that our theology is mostly male. It doesn't necessarily work for women.

Until the mid-1970s, when female theologians like Letty Russell, Rosemary Ruether, Elisabeth Schüssler Fiorenza, Elaine Pagels, and others[25] began publishing, the very nature of the theological enterprise was based on white male systems and ideas. Traditionally, theology has been derived systematically in the male style, by a very careful analysis of ideas, a construction, often in minute detail, of "what's right," and an assumption that the most important thing in one's faith is to know God or to think about God in the right way. This systematic process "begins with authoritative sources and works through to some kind of application, supposedly allowing little room for human experience," as one clergywoman describes it. Certainly there's been no room for women's experience. And when women began constructing theology, they were at first most criticized for including their own experience in it.

But wait. Traditional theologies also incorporate patriarchal notions of the supremacy of the male, making sexism appear the normative nature of human relations, the order of creation, and the relation of God to humanity and history.[26] In other words, traditional theology has valued men's experience but has passed it off as reality. That's the nature of the prevailing paradigm, remember. It surrounds us so that we think that its constructs are universal. The truth is somewhat different. The truth is, "There was always a theology of experience," a laywoman and theologian points out. "Experience is nothing new in theology. It was just male experience. Theology has always been about experience, but now the experiences are changing. And so are the people writing theology."

Feminist theologians are contributing to the theological debate in ways that are useful to both women and men. Their theologies shed the light of day on the long-accepted sexual bias of orthodox Christian theologies and engage in a systematic reconstruction of human relationships to God with a new paradigm—the full personhood of woman, and the intention to manifest a vision of human redemption outside patriarchy.[27] This is the shift "from an androcentric to a feminist perception of the world and . . . the shift also from apologetic focus on biblical authority to articulation of contemporary women's experience."[28] Feminist theologies develop a spiral of action and reflection, a method that "assumes that we all express our theology, our understanding of how God is at work in our lives by our language, thought, and actions."[29] Feminist reflection is not alone in valuing human experience as a resource for theology. However, it is distinctive in its special identification of the lived experience of women.[30]

One woman recalls her first encounter with feminist theology in this way: "I never knew anything out there could touch me so deeply. I really had a hunger, a thirst. I knew I'd been searching for something that's more than what I get (in church) on a regular basis."

Not only feminist theologians, but also clergywomen and other women in church leadership are challenging the assumptions of orthodox (male) theologies, simply by virtue of the way in which they go about their ministry. Increasingly, the carefully constructed theologies of the white male system are challenged by women who demonstrate that their experience, too, is a part of theology. Contemporary women hope that feminist theologies finally provide them an opportunity to engage in the theological enterprise without "the loss of their own perspective and culture in order to do 'good (orthodox) theology.' " Feminist theology creates a passionate bond among women, across denominational lines, because the truth of the gospel has for so long seemed to them threatened by theologies and practices that legitimize man's domination over women.[31] Women respond to feminist theologies first by saying, if even quietly to themselves: "Finally!"

Though many men are thoughtful about feminist theology, and find in it some useful perspectives, the response to women developing theology is, in balance, most often negative in the masculine environment of the denominations. Women still too often "pay the price of being marginalized or pushed out of the thinking and life of the church."[32] They are attacked directly for heretical theology, shallow thinking, or other supposed academic shortfalls. Even the denominations or individual congregations that employ them are attacked for "becoming less theologically sound." Women can readily give examples of vicious criticism of their theology.

"One reaction is that our deviation from the norm is so outrageous that it's heretical, and we need to be disciplined and brought back into line. From my point of view, it's a witchhunt, an attempt to suppress dissent and stamp out deviancy. The claim underlying it is that women are not allowed to do theology. We don't have the right," says one churchwoman, adding: "In theology, as in all leadership, women will not be given the room to make mistakes that men have."

Feminist theologies are not all alike, to be sure. They "articulate the feminine paradigm in different ways with the help of varying philosophical perspectives."[33] They also have some weaknesses, as does any theology.[34] And there is a danger inherent in labeling them as well, warns a female theologian: "I have even often argued that the term 'feminist theology' is a creation of the patriarchy, to kind of capture it and encapsulate it." Her point: By naming and putting boundaries around women doing theology, men might be able to limit its influence.

The implication of all such criticism is obvious: "Now that we have women in our ranks, we can no longer construct a male system theology, and that isn't right." At the basis of this rejection is not hate for women. It is an inability to understand that women's experience is a valid component of theology. But so long as the denominations remain fundamentally masculine, this will not change much. Women's theology will remain suspect.

And What About Paul?

When I asked the question: "Does theology work against women?" many women assumed I was talking about the apostle Paul. Within the fundamentalist movement in particular, Paul presents unique theological concerns that still lurk, preventing women from taking a central role in leadership in their churches and (if one would believe what is written) even in their own families, regardless of their ability. Paul's concerns have less to do with women's own views about theology and more to do with whether the women should ever be allowed to express those views. We cannot depart from a discussion of how theology affects women without dealing with Paul.

Much is written about Paul and his views of women. So much is written, in fact, that legitimate debate about women in leadership, particularly in the neoevangelical denominations, is drowned by a sea of discourse. It's too much; and it will never be resolved by more. Papers, essays, speeches, even books have been written about what Paul said or meant by what he said: Should women veil their heads to acknowledge their subordination? Did Paul allow women to play

leadership roles in the early church? Was Paul more antiwoman than
Jesus? Why did Paul say "In Christ there is no male or female" if he
also meant that women should be silent and subordinate? What does
he mean by "the husband is head of the wife"? Did Paul say that women
should have no authority over men, or was that someone else, writing
in Paul's stead?[35] Was Paul against makeup and fancy dress, or assertive
women? What are Paul's guidelines for the proper marriage relationship? What was Paul's real concern about marriage? How much does
context, social custom, and situation matter in how we read Paul?

The list could go on. It is endless. I do not mean to dismiss Paul,
but to suggest that the debate about Paul will never be resolved in favor
of the leadership of women in the church so long as the denominations
remain so masculine. This is particularly true in the radically masculine
environment of the neoevangelicals. Only when the paradigm changes
can we engage in fruitful discussion about Paul's wisdom on the
leadership of women, in both the home and the church. Until then,
women seem best off answering as did Carolyn Arness who, in an
interview for a pastoral call, was questioned about 1 Timothy 2:11-12.
She said, "I really don't know for certain how to interpret (that text).
It just may be that on judgment day I will have to answer for violating
what is said there. But I am willing to take my medicine." She adds:
"That is not the only text in the Bible. There are hundreds, even
thousands of other pages in that book. I try to listen to what is said on
them all. For example, at the end of the Gospel of Matthew, Jesus says,
'Go therefore and make disciples of all nations, baptizing them in the
name of the Father, and of the Son, and of the Holy Spirit, teaching
them to obey everything that I have commanded you.' Well, somebody
needs to go and do that. Somebody needs to teach our children about
the love of Jesus. Somebody needs to call us to discipleship. Somebody
needs to baptize. And in my heart I believe God has called me to do
just those things."[36]

Clergywomen and other women working in the church must deal
with all of the biases of the business world, but in addition to that, they
face the biases of the church against women in leadership. Women
themselves report that when prejudice against their participation is
covert and theologically justified, it is much harder to overcome, much
more psychologically painful, and much harder to live with. It's one
thing for women to hear that they "don't fit in." It's intolerable for

women working in the church to hear that even God thinks that they're inferior members of the Body of Christ. But as long as the denominations remain fundamentally masculine, women will continue to be marginalized by their biology, and their theology will not be taken seriously, no matter how legitimate it is on its own terms.

Language and What We Believe

If theology orders what we believe, language expresses it, with symbols we call words. It's simple. What we say reflects what we believe. Women, wishing fervently to be known, call for language that images them and reflects their participation in the work of the church. This requires a reexamination of language about God, language about ourselves, and language about our denominations. I cannot put it more powerfully than the churchwoman who said, "I don't think that an equal number of feminine images of God would appease me. We need a diversity, a wealth of images for God, and some we can't even imagine that are beyond our comprehension. Second, I would distinguish between language used for God and language we use for ourselves. Here, we desperately need to be inclusive. Finally, language isn't simply gendered; it is also power laden and it can mask or unmask power relations. I for one am frightened by how much my church organization uses language that masks power."

Unfortunately, in the environment of our denominations, as in our culture, many forces work together to ensure that language reflects the masculine. My object here is not to argue for more feminine images of God or to plead for more inclusive language in everyday discourse, or even to unmask the power relations behind our language. Others have done that eloquently.[37] My point is to show what happens to language in an environment that is sexualized to be masculine.

Let us begin with God. When I was a junior in high school, the young woman who sat behind me in English class was a devout Jew. I noticed that her word for the divine was G-d. I once asked her why, and I have never forgotten the answer she gave me: Because, she said "we believe that we cannot name God." God is not only beyond our gender defining, but also beyond our naming *at all*. But we seem to be bereft of images that help us see God in anything but masculine or feminine, mother or father terminology. In most cases we cannot even get beyond the masculine to feminine images of God,[38] and when we do, we seem somehow incapable of imaging the whole of God, assigning instead "dimensions of God" to the feminine. In a masculine environment, our language about God will persist in reflecting a man-God. And yes, it is true that our human limitations and our dualistic habits then cause us to think of God as male—and even to think of the male as more like God than the female. This is what women object to. But it remains my contention that women's arguments will bear little fruit so long as the denominations remain fundamentally masculine. Why is this so?

The answer lies in a careful look at what happens to our religious language in a masculine environment. First, feminine language for God is seen politically—as God-imaging that merely "promotes the psychological and social emancipation of women." At the same time, the heavily masculine language of the Bible is *not* seen politically. Instead it is understood to provide "connectors *to the reality of God* that transcend our images and language."[39] There is a double standard here built into the prevailing paradigm of masculinity, which allows both men and women to hear male language as neutral and female language as gender-biased.

A second and related phenomenon is the way in which feminine images from original source materials become masculine in translation. Consider Deuteronomy 32:18 as just one example. In *The Jerusalem Bible* it reads: "You forget the rock who begot you, unmindful now of the God who fathered you."[40] The words "fathered you" are translated from the Hebrew which literally means "writhing in labor," a womanly image if ever there was one. In *The Jerusalem Bible*, however, translation makes the image thoroughly masculine and patriarchal.[41]

Third, any call for more feminine images in our religious language, whether it comes from men or women, is greeted with suspicion and often ridicule. Someone can always think of an awkward example that makes changing language "impossible." And so the debate goes on endlessly, with no resolution in sight. As a result we create the fourth problem for ourselves. We are never able to rise above our gender dualism to a multitude of images for God.

And what about us? What about the way we use language to talk about ourselves? This also falls victim to human limitations peculiar to the masculine environment. First, the masculine becomes normative in our speech, and is actually written into our rules of grammar. Our habit of using masculine pronouns reminds us constantly that men are active in human history. Women are less visible, sometimes invisible. I myself used to accept the grammatical conventions that made it so. The pronoun "he" stands for both male and female, but "she" does not. In classical English grammar that is the rule. But if I can see beyond the masculine biases that made the rules that way, I can then observe that using "he" to talk about humanity works in favor of men and contributes to the invisibility of women. This reality causes one woman to ask: "How many 'him hymns' are legitimate? How many kings and how many fathers can we sing about before we circumscribe our understanding of the very nature of God?"[42] It plays subtly on our subconscious, imaging men for us all the time, women seldom.

There are no easy solutions in English grammar, especially with pronouns, but surely there are ways to be linguistically more inclusive of women more of the time. Doing so consistently would not only image women in important ways, but would also help to break down the subconscious but stubbornly masculine bias of our social interaction. Doing so consistently is also a constant challenge in a masculine environment, like swimming upstream against a hard current.

In fact, our everyday language is so limited by an overabundance of male metaphors and images and derivatives that we hardly see them anymore. This is a second problem for our common speech. How often are we aware that the word for our theological schools—seminary—is a derivative of the Latin *semen*, meaning seed. Basically masculine stuff! How often do we notice that our workaday language engages us in strategies and task forces, which bring to mind military images, also masculine imaging for the warrior world. There are a thousand more examples.

Power is the other language issue of the denominations. Language can be used, and often is used by denominations to mask power, to give power, or to establish who has power. The first problem here is that our language reflects a hierarchical world in which there are dominants and subordinates. Hierarchical language establishes who has power and who does not, in its style, word choices, meaning, and clarity. Subordinates are often assigned descriptors with pejorative meaning, revealing our prejudices as well as how we see the hierarchy arranged. One well-known example of this phenomenon is the way in which the word black and 60 of its 120 synonyms have come to be associated with negative meaning, causing the late Martin Luther King, Jr. to observe that "even semantics have conspired to make that which is black seem ugly and degrading."[43] The same happens to women. The extremely pejorative meaning of the word "bitch" is but one example.

Further, the language of our organizations typically masks power relationships. Passive voice in our denominational language ("It has been decided that . . .") never tells who is doing what, and thereby masks power with a grammatical construction. It is weak language, as any writer or grammarian knows, but it's the typical style of organizations, including denominations. "Passive voice doesn't say who is in charge, who expects what, who is making the decisions. It masks the authority figures," insists one laywoman, a theologian. And it doesn't work in any collaborative environment. But in our hierarchies, it is habit, a bad habit.

That language confuses us, puts off our ability to see our women as leaders, forces us in our human limitation to image God as male, is obvious. We might end up as confused as the little girl who asked in a prayer, "Dear God, are boys better than girls? I know you are one, but try to be fair."[44] Better that we should be like the little boy who, when asked by his clergy mom what God is like, replied: "I think God is more like both of us."

Women in church leadership hope that the sexuality of the denominations might become less masculine so that a view such as this boy's might prevail, a theology including women's experience might be taken seriously, and feminine sexuality might be honored as its own miracle, rather than feared and hated.

Part Two

Leadership Traps

Organizational Wives or New Paradigm Leaders?

When Jesus visited the home of Mary and Martha, Mary sat at his feet intent upon his teaching. Martha bustled about tending to the hospitality that an honored guest deserved. We have long thought of this as a story of two women, one who "chose the better part," and the other who was overly absorbed in her housekeeping. Surely, in a literal sense, this is the story of two women. It is also, in my view, the story of one woman. It reminds women that there is a Mary and a Martha in each of us. We do feel called to "take care of" others in the workplace and at home. This may be the result of socialization. We also long to sit, like Mary, at the feet of the Master, ignoring the housekeeping and concerning ourselves with the other tasks of leadership. Jesus affirmed a woman's desire to put aside the housekeeping chores and take on other leadership tasks when he said, "Martha, you are worried and distracted by many things; there is need of only one thing. Mary has chosen the better part, which will not be taken away from her" (Luke 10:41-42).

Women fervently hope that they will be welcomed as leaders, and not relegated to the housekeeping of the denominations. Some modern-day observers believe that women's hope will be realized. Women in the next century will benefit in the workplace, they say, because their leadership style is unique and needed. They argue that women will be able to use their unique style to transform organizations. Ann Huff, a professor of business administration and observer of women in the workplace, disagrees. She argues that women working in a male system merely become "organizational wives" relegated to the repetitious "housekeeping" chores of administration.[1] The very feminine leadership styles that others[2] claim will help women are the styles that Huff says will trap them instead—an ability to be people-centered, encouraging of others, deferential to the success of groups rather than themselves, negotiating rather than forceful, networking rather than hierarchical. There's a little bit of mothering in the mix here too. It's a fact, as women leaders know, that "the world turns to women for mothering, and this fact silently attaches itself to many a job description."[3] The point: "organization wives [or mothers] not only exhaust themselves, they behave in ways that keep them at lower levels in their profession. They deny themselves, and are denied by their organizations, the experiences that will allow them to rise to the top."[4] As one woman put it: "Women even in senior positions tend to be placed in the helper roles, doing the detail work, and men tend to be regarded as broad thinkers." Nuechterlein and Hahn describe how this happens to women in parish ministry, citing the example of a female pastor who "recognizes that she, as a woman, has been culturally conditioned to be actively involved in service projects and behind-the-scenes church work that have called forth sociomotive roles." She recognizes that she has not been encouraged to take on masculine roles and be a leader of church groups or churches.[5] This is a good description of the Mary-Martha dilemma. Every woman struggles with it. We are socialized to take on the housekeeping chores of the church, and at the same time we yearn to participate in the other tasks of leadership.

Huff's prediction is chilling for every woman leader, in the church or out. It is based on the assumption that women will continue to work within the hierarchical paradigm, and therefore, their style will be used against them. Literally, it will "keep them in their place."

She has a point, if we are honest about what happens to women in leadership. On the one hand, women are expected to be like men if they want to succeed. But, the more they do act like men, the more they are criticized. This happens because women are not judged by the same criteria, even when they adopt the hierarchical leadership paradigm. On the other hand, if women try to work as women, assuming they will be judged on the merits of what we might call the collaborative or "embracing" paradigm, they are considered weak and ineffective, or as Huff predicts and Neuchterlein and Hahn illustrate, they are "relegated to the role of organizational or church wife."

The female manager who was considered too assertive by her denomination's board, and the young laywoman who sought ordination after many successful years in campus ministry,[6] got caught in the "you're too bitchy" trap. This is a trap laid by the rules of the white male paradigm that state: women should not be angry (or even assertive, because this reminds us of anger). One woman we interviewed puts it this way: "There are two extremes. You have to assert yourself or you are too quiet; but if you assert yourself too much, you are too bold." Miriam found this out when, together with her brother Aaron she cried out, "Has the LORD spoken only through Moses? Has he not spoken through us also?" (Numbers 12:1). For her impertinence Miriam was struck with leprosy, while her brother Aaron was left unpunished.

There are other traps for women working in the white male system, which they encounter "not only because of sexism in their denominations and congregations, but also because their practice of ministry has moved away from the old patriarchal models."[7] The fact is, "women may not fit comfortably into patriarchal models of leadership. Either they will not be effective leaders because they are unable to be effective 'fathers,' or they will find themselves uncomfortable with the incongruence between a role as defined by men and their authentic self."[8]

> **THEME FIVE:**
> **Women work as immigrants in a foreign land.**

Women are "the resident Other in Western culture. We are the opposite of all that is normal. We are aliens, strangers, the permanent *ex-matriates.*"[9] Because women are immigrants, we do not fit, cannot fit, and will be "trapped" unwittingly by the rules of the culture that we do not know. Like the immigrants from other cultures who swamped the shores of the United States in the late nineteenth and early twentieth centuries, women struggle to learn a new language and a different way of doing things. And like those immigrants, we urge our offspring— our daughters—to learn the language and the ways of the dominant culture better than we have.

As men struggle to learn to work with us, they too encounter traps, though to a lesser extent. Men are creators and beneficiaries of the

dominant paradigm, but when they encounter women in significant
numbers, paradigms clash, chaos follows, and even the men encounter
some surprises. Again, think of the immigration patterns in our country as a point of comparison. Until very recently, non-English speaking
people had to blend into the dominant culture of the United States.
But now that too is changing. Already, there are enough Hispanic
people in the United States that European American people begin to
think about the necessity of learning to speak Spanish. It's just one
example of how a dominant culture breaks down when the numbers
shift. Now consider again the white male paradigm, and how it breaks
down around the edges as more and more women come into leadership.

In her landmark book *Men and Women of the Corporation*, Rosabeth
Moss Kanter argues that the makeup of the group strongly influences
the tensions and stresses faced by individual members of the group.
She defines groups in terms of the ratio between two significant social
categories (for our purposes, women and men). A uniform group would
have all women or all men. Skewed groups would have a large group
of dominants (men) and up to 15 percent women. Tilted groups would
have 20 to 35 percent women and the rest men. Balanced groups would
have a 60:40 ratio or half of each sex. The traps experienced here are
more likely to affect the minority sex, the more severely the group is
unbalanced.[10] For example, a woman in a skewed group is more likely
to experience the traps for women than a woman in a balanced group.

The stories in part 2 are meant to illustrate the common traps faced
primarily by women, and to a lesser extent by men as paradigms
change. They were shared in a spirit of hopefulness that new paradigms
more satisfying to both men and women might emerge.[11]

Chapter Six

The Incredible, Invisible Woman

N o matter what position they hold, women in church leadership cite the invisibility traps as the most common and perhaps the most frustrating. These include "What Does It Feel Like?" "The Invisible Woman," and "Whose Idea Was It?" All of these traps have something to do with a woman's lack of visibility and the resulting consequences. These are the traps that women reportedly get caught in nearly every day. Eventually women begin to wonder if they are really seen at all.

What Does It Feel Like?

When Suzanne was elected the first female bishop in her denomination in the U.S. she had only one complaint: "I wish someone would ask me about the issues." The only comment solicited from her was: "What does it feel like to be the first woman bishop?" Suzanne recognizes the need to speak for all women, but she adds, there are many more important issues in the church. She could talk about those as well as her male colleagues, but she will seldom be asked.

The first trap for women working in a male system is that gender is always the main issue. It is never quite possible for a woman to overcome the insinuation that she got the job "because she is a woman." If her denomination has a quota system, this is particularly true. Beyond that, people always want first to know what it feels like "for a woman to work here." When she demonstrates that she is actually able to talk intelligently about other things, she surprises people. Another woman in denominational service puts it this way: "I thought when they made this big deal about having a certain percentage of women here, they had some expectation of what that was going to mean—that there would be the intention to include women in decision-making circles . . . and that has never, never happened."

When women fall into this trap they become "zoo exhibits," representatives of a species rather than individual people with hopes and dreams.[1] Thus, United Methodist clergywoman Marian Coger adds, when a woman succeeds or fails it is often interpreted to mean something about all women's ability to succeed or tendency to fail.[2]

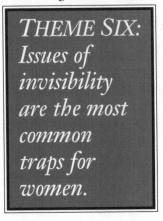

THEME SIX: Issues of invisibility are the most common traps for women.

This kind of tokenism is stressful for women for three critical reasons. First, it makes them representative of all women, and not individuals. Women may recognize the need to be "firsts," even to fill quotas if necessary. They understand simple arithmetic. "Women have to be there in greater numbers before things will change," says one. But the experience of being a number is not necessarily a pleasant one. It can make women doubt themselves: "I was one of the first women available," one woman remembers, "and I was nearly tokened to death for awhile. That made me very unsure of whether I had anything to offer aside from gender." It denies a woman's opportunity to speak as an individual: "I cannot raise questions in public about the quota system," complains one woman, "because the minute I do I get singled out as 'the feminist who doesn't believe in quotas.'" It can exact a tremendous physical toll: "I am expected to do the same amount of speaking, writing, teaching, committee work as my [male] colleagues, but I am also expected to represent my institution at every turn. We want our women to be high profile, but we won't hire enough women to do all the representational work." So the few who are there are run ragged.

One aspect of this tension is what Marian Coger calls "notoriety," the tendency for the clergywoman (and I would say, also, the laywoman in church leadership), to "be singled out and held up as an example of extraordinariness."[3] "There's something about being in a position of visibility, where a lot of people look to you as an example that I didn't like," says another, with great candor and thoughtfulness, after leaving a church leadership position. "It's like you are a number and not a person anymore. The men want to know 'what it's like' and the women put all their hopes and dreams on you in a way that's not fair for them or for you." Almost every element of the woman's job may include elements of being "singled out," Coger warns. And though this can be a source of growth, it can also "exact a psychic toll."[4] The themes of isolation, marginality, and notoriety "create an image of the managerial women as high-wire artists. They live in the spotlight, highly visible, very much alone up there." It can be heady and very uncomfortable. With all eyes focused on oneself, the woman realizes that she "has not been told all one needs to know to stay up on the high wire."[5]

It's easy to see how this trap puts pressure on women to overachieve, lest they give off the message that "women can't hack it."[6] This is its second stress. "One of my temptations is to be a model, and I am tempted to push my church to be a model as well. I want us to be models so we can show the world that it can be done . . . But neither I nor the church is called to be a model for anyone else. We are called to be faithful to God's unique call to us. A by-product of our faithfulness might be that other people on the path look to us and are encouraged. But this is God's business, not ours."[7]

This clergywoman and her colleagues may have the most intense struggle here for a variety of reasons. The tendency for clergy workaholism affects both men and women, but there are additional stresses for women. It is still likely that the female pastor is the *only* clergywoman the people in her parish have ever met. Even if this is not the case, the clergywoman struggles to prove herself capable on behalf of all others at the same time that she works against the prevailing attitude, verified by recent studies, that "there is a general incompatibility between the image of minister and that of woman."[8]

Third, and finally, this trap makes women the visible targets for the pain, confusion, and grief that men and women feel over their changing roles in society at large.[9] The emergence of women in church leadership is a factor in changing paradigms within our society. Often unwittingly, women become paradigm shifters. They will be the targets of a great deal of powerful and potentially destructive anger and blame from those around them who stand to benefit most from the existing paradigms—both women and men.

One articulate clergywoman sums it up this way: "I struggle with particular pressures today. The historical moment has placed woman pastors in a spotlight that can be blinding. We and our work are under magnifying glass scrutiny. And when I speak I am still resisting the centuries old gravity that works to pull women back into their seats and to keep them silent and smiling. When I speak I also sense solidarity with an invisible cloud of women witnesses who are standing with me and begging me to break the sound barrier for them too. It is a wonder—one of God's wonders—that any of us attempt to be pastors at all."[10]

The Invisible Woman

In one large congregation, the women on staff—both lay and clergy—have agreed to wear bright colors to staff meetings. Following through on this decision was expensive for some of the women who had to buy a new suit in red or bright blue or even yellow. All felt it was worth it. The goal for these women was to increase the number of times they had the opportunity to speak in the meetings. Early on in their experience, these women, who represent about 15 percent of the group, realized that their "floor time" was minimal. Their complaints led to a consultant analysis of the group dynamic, which verified what the women experienced. Of the half dozen women in the group, only one emerged statistically as a frequent speaker. In contrast, there were many men among the frequent speakers.

One outcome of this trap is that women remain invisible. No matter how good their ideas, how often they themselves create opportunities to share ideas, or how often or how vocally they speak up in meetings, they remain invisible. In a similar group setting, a woman recalls presenting a complicated plan for group consideration. She was backed up by an influential male in the group. Discussion followed for about thirty minutes, during which time many questions were asked about the plan. Afterwards, in debriefing the discussion, the woman who had presented the plan pointed out to the men that they had asked all their questions about the plan of the man who backed her up. Not once was she asked, by a man in the discussion, anything about the plan she was responsible to research, formulate, and present to the group. The men reacted to this feedback in three ways. Some who recognized the criticism accepted it, though they were silent in their acceptance.

Others saw nothing wrong with their behavior and queried her defensively with the question, "What's wrong with that?" Still others denied the feedback altogether.

Women in church leadership positions frequently cite this trap as a source of constant frustration. Perhaps the most common form of this trap is the countless number of times that women put forth an idea only to have it ignored, brought up later by a man, and suddenly heard by others in the group. As a result, women feel voiceless. One woman describes it this way: "If you're in a group setting, and you make a suggestion or you come up with an idea or a plan, they go on to something else. Then a man says it in his own words twenty minutes later and suddenly it's a bright idea."

Even a published author can run into this problem, though it seems that it would be difficult for men to ignore something as tangible as the printed word. "I am known to be an avid gardener, and the men in my profession ask me only about that. They want to establish a personal connection with me, not a professional one. They have seen my articles, my books, but they never ask about that. It's always and only my gardening," the woman, a theologian, reports. "Their way of relating to me personally becomes a way to discount me as a scholar. To me, it is shocking."

Why shocking? "For many women, being is intimately connected with being heard," say Neuchterlein and Hahn.[11] And it's no wonder. Research shows that people—both women and men—take men more seriously as speakers and do not hear women as well as they hear men. Men, socialized to be experts, "often can hear only their own voice."[12] Women have more difficulty than men in asserting their authority, considering themselves authorities, expressing themselves in public so that others will listen, gaining others' respect for their intellect and ideas, and fully using their capability and training in their work. As a result, they often end up feeling unheard even when they have something important to say.[13]

This is not necessarily because women aren't capable, intelligent, or forceful speakers. It's because a man's way of asserting himself as an authority in conversation is the norm, and therefore the standard by which we judge women as well. Deborah Tannen, in her landmark book *You Just Don't Understand*, explains three critical points among the many conversational styles she researches so intricately.

First, she documents what female church leaders experience in their staff meetings—that it is very difficult for women to get the chance to speak. Men, she says, tend to "need someone to listen and agree" with their point of view or their explanations. Women comply by being the listeners. But, she adds, women get negatively judged for their choice. Their decision to be the listeners is judged as indecisiveness and insecurity, a reflection that they are, indeed, less knowledgeable, less secure in their opinions, and less skilled at speaking. The real reason women often defer: to be polite, to be considerate of the other speaker—the man.[14] Indeed, women frequently reported in interviews the feeling of "being had" in encounters like this. They listen politely, defer to male speakers, even those who interrupt them, and in the end they are perceived to be insecure or inarticulate rather than simply polite.

Tannen gives an exhausting and careful analysis of the phenomenon of interrupting as well. "Men who approach conversation as a contest are likely to expend effort not to support the other's talk but to lead the conversation in another direction, perhaps one in which they can take center stage . . . But in doing so they expect their conversational partners to mount resistance. Women who yield to these efforts do so not because they are weak or insecure or deferential, but because they have little experience in deflecting attempts to grab the conversational wheel. They see steering the conversation in a different direction not as a game, but as a violation of the rules of the game."[15] What's most important to remember is the different goals men and women have in a conversation. Men tend to approach a conversation as a contest. Women tend to approach it as a connection. But remember the paradigms! Because white men have set the prevailing paradigm of our culture, women and all minorities get judged by the white man's standard for approaching conversations, not their own.

More troubling even than this is Tannen's finding that women in conversation get judged more harshly than men, even when they *do* converse in the same way. She cites studies of tag questions, statements with little questions added to the end of sentences (It's a nice day, isn't it?). Women, she says, are expected to use more tag questions in conversation than men. Even when men and women use the same number of tag questions in conversation, she adds, women are judged less knowledgeable and intelligent than men who also use them. Furthermore, "women who do not give supporting evidence for their arguments are judged less intelligent and knowledgeable, *but men who advanced arguments without support were not.*"[16]

Here's how this plays out. Women's ideas are not taken as seriously. They are not asked for advice by their male colleagues nearly as often as men ask one another for advice. And often, women will experience men asking one another for further information about an idea or report that originally came from a woman. Over time, these kinds of experiences make women wonder if they are really invisible to the men around them. What's really happening is that others around them, especially the men, cannot relate to the women's way of talking or interacting. The women are not literally invisible, of course, but their voices are often unheard and their leadership style is usually misunderstood as well. This is hard for women to take, when all they really want is for their ministry, their leadership, to be taken seriously.[17]

Whose Idea Was It?

Some years ago, when Hannah's denomination conducted building-wide office renovations, another female manager approached Hannah with a problem. She was unable to get the all-male building remodeling team to take her office design seriously. It seemed that the remodeling in her division would never get done, because they were telling her what to do, and she had other ideas. Hannah's unit, on the other hand, had not only succeeded in being remodeled, it had moved to another location in the building where the remodeling plan could be carried out better. Hannah's female colleague asked her "how she did it." Simple, Hannah replied. When the remodeling team wouldn't listen to her, she assigned the project to one of the male staff members in her department. The change in attitude was instantaneous, and before she knew it, all of Hannah's ideas for the new space became a reality.

This strategy is typically embraced by women working in a white male system. It's a way of finally getting something done. Savvy women know that they need men around them to get anything done. It's not because they or their female staff are not competent. It's because the male system thrives on white male style. The trap is that women are forced to "give up" their ideas to men in order to move their organization or their objectives forward. In the end, the women lose because the men get the credit for their ideas or their work.

Women (and some men who "give up" their ideas to other men) will get out of this trap only when the white male system breaks down enough to allow more collaborative paradigms for leadership to be recognized and appreciated. In the meantime, women face this trap routinely. Some find humor in the fact that men will take on their good ideas, take credit for them, and not even have the awareness to realize what they have done. One woman, a well-respected volunteer leader in her denomination is matter-of-fact about it: "I think we have to be above board in everything we do. I've never had a hidden agenda. I've never tried to play a game to get what I want. I've never manipulated to get what I want. I must say, a lot of times I've thrown an idea out and it wasn't picked up, but by the time the meeting ended, it was what they were doing, and the men took full credit for it." Later she added, "I don't care, so long as it gets done."

Other women do care—a lot. Having their ideas taken over by a man is as much a violation to them as having their written word plagiarized. It seems to them unethical.

Why does it happen? Sexism is one reason. Another, says Rosabeth Kanter, is the quest for power or power alignments. Both males and females within the white male system want to align themselves with the leader who has power, because within the prevailing paradigm, power brings reward. Kanter defines power as the ability to get things done, mobilize resources, and access whatever is needed to move ahead. In the corporation (and Coger argues, in the church as well), effective leadership requires competence and power. An effective leader has to have more than good ideas. She has to have the ability to turn ideas into action. This requires power in the white male paradigm. It follows, then, that most people want to work for or align themselves with a leader who has power. That usually means men, because men are perceived to have more power.[18] The bottom line: people are more likely to put their bets on men as winners because they doubt how far women can go, and they believe women cannot bring anyone (else) along.[19]

When clergywomen or other female leaders hear the complaint that "things will fall apart if we have a woman in charge," they are hearing a bias that women lack power. When they hear the comment "Ministry is becoming a woman's profession" as a complaint, they are hearing the voice of someone who assumes that ministry will become a less powerful profession. After all, Coger points out, effective leadership in the white male paradigm requires credibility, competence, and power. "Clergywomen [and I would add, other female leaders in the church] may prove repeatedly that they are competent, but at this time in our society and within the church, they are perceived to be less powerful."[20] Indeed, because women are working in a system that does not welcome them, it is often true that they have less access to power than their male colleagues.[21]

Being Invisible

When a woman is invisible, she does not exist. She cannot make a difference. In fact, she cannot have a ministry, be a minister, or be a leader. She cannot do anything because she does not exist. Three extreme examples come to mind that will illustrate the extent of this problem for professional women. In the Southern Baptist Church, there are no denominational records kept of women clergy. Records are kept by Dr. Sarah Frances Anders, working as a sociologist of religion. She advocates the importance of knowing what is happening to women in her denomination. In the United Church of Christ, one clergywoman who has been in her parish two years has yet to see her name added to the congregation's letterhead or signboard. And in the Assemblies of God, discussion about women's role in the leadership of a new extension college was wiped from the official record of the constitutional proceedings. Not only were women, by implication, not welcome in leadership, but there would be no historical record of the fact that anyone ever asked.[22]

The overall effect of these traps is that they render women invisible and therefore incapable of doing. Of course, women literally exist. We see them all around us. We who are women see ourselves in the mirror. But women cannot function as active persons in the paradigm if they are rendered invisible there. When this happens there is loss on both sides. For women, there is deep personal loss on a psychic level. For the church, there is loss of talent and possibility.

Chapter Seven

The Cinderella Syndrome

Women who want to advance must work very hard. Many men work very hard too, of course. But the result is different. Men who work hard—so the ethic goes—can count on rewards for doing so: praise, advancement, even fame and wealth, all the trappings of success. Women cannot expect the same outcome for their hard work, because of three traps: "Make Me Comfortable," "Work Twice as Hard," and "The Better You Do . . . ". These traps illustrate that women who work hard may actually be punished for doing so, because men are uncomfortable with their success.

Make Me Comfortable

After three years as associate pastor in a large congregation, Betty's committees were the most active and the most productive in the parish. The senior pastor suggested a reshuffling of the committee assignments among the staff. A third pastor, a male associate, younger and less experienced than Betty, supported the change, but Betty did not. Eventually, the senior pastor made an autocratic decision, informing Betty and the male associate of new committee assignments. Betty found that she had lost all of her active committees to the men with whom she worked. Betty was stunned by the move, and confronted the senior pastor. He relented, giving her back one of her former committees. As a result of her objection, Betty endured several years of professional harassment from her senior pastor before she finally left the congregation for another call. The harassment confused and angered Betty. She was, after all, only setting her boundaries when she objected. The senior pastor, on the other hand, interpreted her to be making a power move against him, and he reacted accordingly—and appropriately from his point of view.

One might wonder if this congregation in general is making a mistake by thinking that church committees actually do ministry. Most church committees are notorious hollow shells, and Betty was out to change that as she liberated volunteers to start doing ministry instead of chatting about it. Betty's immediate mistake was that she failed to observe one of the cardinal rules of the white male system: men need to feel comfortable at all times, and it is the job of others around them, including women above them in the system, to keep them comfortable. A laywoman in church management summarizes her experience this way: "I continue to get promoted not only because I am productive. It's also because I do my work and don't make any trouble. But you can be sure that anytime I break even the smallest rule, I am reprimanded thoroughly." This woman's comment illustrates what all women in leadership know very well. It is their job to keep the men feeling comfortable. If they don't, they risk retaliation that can be surprising, brutal, and swift.

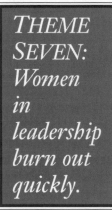

THEME SEVEN: Women in leadership burn out quickly.

Women make men at the top feel uncomfortable when they break the rules of the white male paradigm. There are so many ways a woman can do this that the workplace is like a minefield. Betty is an example of a woman setting her own boundaries, and making a man feel uncomfortable by doing so. Women also make men feel uncomfortable when their style is different, when they state a point of view that threatens the prevailing paradigm, when they do well, or just because they are female and they are there. In the interview setting, women demonstrated their ability to recall countless examples of each of these situations. Let's look at a few more.

Having a different style: Many women report being judged "ineffective at getting things done" because they have a different style than their male peers. What's really happening? A man feels uncomfortable because the woman's style is different and unfamiliar to his way of working. He may, in fact, literally not be able to understand how the woman is getting anything done. Attorney General Janet Reno took hits for her style in just this way. Acknowledged as one of the most successful members of President Clinton's cabinet, she was still losing credit for her success to her male staff because her leadership style was misunderstood.[1]

Stating a threatening point of view: To illustrate how women may make men feel uncomfortable by stating a threatening point of view, consider what happens to those who advocate the use of feminine images of God.[2] Women who do this are often attacked, professionally maligned and discredited, and called names. Why? They are challenging the centrality of maleness and men in our culture and our belief system.

In the next section of this chapter we shall discuss in greater detail the fourth way women make men feel uncomfortable—by **being too effective.** And then, there is fifth, the one no woman can avoid: **being female.** Deborah Sheppard, Barbara Gutek, Albert Mills, and others have documented, all in separate studies, the effect of being female in management.[3] Sheppard concludes, "for women 'immigrants' moving into male-dominated culture, learning how to manage the world of the organization necessarily implies learning how to redefine and manage 'femaleness.' " This management, she continues, "takes place within a male-defined set of norms and expectations." In order to keep the men comfortable and therefore survive in an alien (white male) paradigm, women in Sheppard's study viewed their gender as something to be managed. "Being a woman in a male-dominated environment demands handling one's gender in particular ways" and is done "with reference to one's interpretation of the prevailing power structure in the organization."[4] It is no different in the church, as any clergywoman can verify.

The issues in this trap are complex. They involve competition, power, security, and the very nature of femaleness. The man who retaliates, like Betty's senior associate did, will not know that he is acting inappropriately if he does not understand the white male system to be only one of a number of possible paradigms for leadership. He may also not know to what extent his discomforts are causing women to deny themselves to survive.

By virtue of the fact that women make male system managers uncomfortable, they are subject to reprimand. It may be only a verbal reprimand from the boss. Betty endured professional harassment. Often it is much more. Women may be the recipients of public criticism for their work, private maneuvering to reduce their authority, or any one of a range of other tactics. In the church, this reprimand may also take a theological spin, as it did with Mary, who was invited to give a paper at a major theological conference hosted by her denomination. One of three speakers, Mary followed a speech by a well known male theologian. Her paper, which was widely judged to be thorough in its research and its presentation, effectively challenged some of his ideas, and the controversy engaged the audience. Some months later, just about the time Mary's paper was accepted for publication, this theologian surprised Mary by publicly claiming that she was "not fit" to be a leader in the church because of what she had written. Mary objected but never received an apology. In fact, Mary was asked to submit her paper to denominational leadership for "review."

There are many examples of theological attacks against women. Witness the recent harassment of Dr. Molly Marshall, a Southern Baptist professor of theology at Southern Seminary in Louisville, Kentucky, until her forced resignation in 1994. Marshall endured ten years of attack by the conservative element in the church before she resigned. During that time, every word she wrote or spoke publicly was scrutinized by her critics who were looking for evidence to use against her. Controversy focused in part on her views of the role of women in ministry, but much of the questioning centered on theological issues such as Dr. Marshall's view of salvation.[5]

Women like Betty, Mary, and Molly are often mystified by the vehemence of the attacks against them. It seems way out of proportion to them because they don't recognize that power is a fundamental value in the white male paradigm, and that all work in that paradigm is a struggle for power. For men operating within the paradigm, a solid grasp of power is the source of their authority. They experience women like Betty or Mary or Molly as threatening their power every time they create discomfort, and these men hold the women responsible for the discomfort they feel. The response of the men is swift and brutal. Cut off her power! Or perhaps it is even more severe, as in Dr. Marshall's case: Get rid of her!

Women rightly fear this retaliation. They work hard, and often unconsciously, to prevent it in at least two ways. First, they try to blend in, and second, they attempt to set their own boundaries in a nonthreatening way. In Sheppard's study, women report their attempt to blend in to the existing organizational culture so as not to cause discomfort for the men. Women may limit their blending by claiming their rightful place in the organization as women, but they largely fear taking a hard-line stand.[6] On the other hand, some women reported success in setting clear boundaries for their work and their style. "If your attitude says, when you really get down to it, 'Don't mess with me,' I think people know that," says one clergywoman. Another stresses, "Underneath all the smiling and the congeniality I stand for what I feel is right and I won't back down." These women and others report that the approach works best when there is a powerful male to back her up, and when she softens her stance with humor. The point remains, however, that no matter what they do, women are still responsible for helping men feel comfortable.

Work Twice as Hard

When one denomination decided to open computer support offices, it hired Susan, a highly competent, experienced laywoman to head the staff. She had a proven track record and was dedicated to her new post. Susan worked long, hard hours. Yet, she could seldom engage her male colleagues in casual conversation, and she had scant informal opportunity to get to know her male colleagues, and thereby enhance the interface of her new department with existing units. After several years of trying, Susan left, stating her frustration openly before her departure. A man was hired to replace her. Within two weeks of his arrival, the other male managers were excited about the opportunity to use new technology and fascinated by all the information he shared.

What Susan experienced was the trap of having to work twice as hard to get half as much done. Women who spoke for this book reported this as well. To one, "there is no such thing as a woman doing the same job [as a man]. She's doing it better," because she has to. "I wouldn't dare go into a meeting and say I hadn't had time" to read the materials. "I do it. I do my homework." Another recalled an incident with a senior staff member who "would not work with me at all until I proved myself. You really do have to prove yourself." This trap is like quicksand for clergy, who also live with the ancient affirmation that pastors are to be "without blemish."[7] Women affirm that drive for perfection: "I probably set standards and expectations for myself that are sometimes unrealistic, and when I don't achieve them and I feel guilty, I think maybe I shouldn't be in this position, not because I am a woman but because I am not good enough," one confesses.

Susan is also an example of how women must struggle in professions that are largely viewed to be men's, because of some notion of skill, which sociologist Albert Mills defines as "a complex of rules about the nature and value of a person's work."[8] Technological fields are popularly thought to be more a man's world, even though large numbers of women are succeeding in them. Consider, for example, the emergence of multimedia children's software in bookstores. The content developers of these products are men, even though nearly all children's book editors and most children's book writers are women. This phenomenon parallels the popular notion that girls are not as good in math as boys.

Mills adds that "a number of factors combine to ensure that skill is rarely attached to the work of females."[9] This has been true historically, and is surely related to our notions about women's ability in the more technical fields such as Susan's. Mills points out that historically, the work of men has been valued more highly. It still is today. Females are rarely recruited to jobs involving traditional skill training. Such training for women is grossly inadequate, and the subsequent cheapening of female labor has been advantageous to employers.[10] Physical strength is another limiting factor for women, often in ways it should not be. Mills documents how our notions of strength in women have historically been used to put them in jobs when they were needed, and to keep them out of jobs when they were not wanted. Susan Faludi illustrates that today, even when women do have the skills or strength for a job that is traditionally male, they can't count on getting the job.[11] Overall, the point: "In any formal organization there is a 'job to be done,' often in a culturally prescribed way, sometimes expressed as 'the way we do things around here.' The various tasks and mode of accomplishing them . . . incorporate assumptions about the nature of men and women; assumptions that are drawn upon and that exclude or undervalue the work of women.[12] The church, no less than any other organization, surely has its gospel of "the way we do things around here!"

Susan also suffered because she didn't have access to the network and therefore the mentors and the decision-making opportunities of her male peers. "To enter, prosper, and survive within an organization can depend upon how a person is viewed by decision makers; whether that person is viewed as a *full* organizational member," Mills points out.[13] He adds, "A variety of organizational practices can signal to females that they are not regarded as full organizational members" including denial of access to important organizational networks, especially around extracurricular activities; lack of availability of mentors for women; and "motivating language of the organization that is couched in male metaphors."[14] One woman I interviewed translates the sociological analysis to practical experience in this way: "You find that very often men will deal with you seriously, but there is a point at which they are more comfortable talking to each other. So, you begin to find out that the real discussions have happened somewhere else." Maybe on the golf course. Maybe in the bathroom.

As if this were not enough, Susan had yet another reason to work twice as hard to get half as much done. She was not accepted by the male peer group because she did not pass their loyalty tests.[15] When acceptance is not forthcoming, the work that women do is thwarted because they are denied access to power in the organization. Furthermore, even when women are granted power, they must continually protect the access they have. Says one manager: "If you can work very, very hard, and if you can live with the charge that you got this job just because you are a woman, and if you can live with the doubts people have about your effectiveness when they observe you leading 'like a woman,' you might succeed. But you will always get reminders that you don't really belong."

These reminders take the form of statements that put women down as a category or that lift women up as an exception. They may also be insults or ridicule of women or women's incompetence, kidding, and off-color jokes told specifically because a token woman is present. The woman is thereby tested and retested by the dominant group to see if she will be loyal to them, by allowing the inappropriateness. At the same time she is tested, she is reminded that ultimately, she is an outsider.[16] Some women find this loyalty testing too difficult to endure and they never become part of the dominant (male) group. They are thereby left without all-important support from male peers. Others who pass the test are better accepted, but run the risk of forgetting what it was like to be an outsider, buying into the white male system, and withdrawing their support and mentoring from other women.

The Better You Do . . .

When Harriet accepted her second call, she moved to a different part of the country. In her new setting, she found that her clergy study group was marginally active and basically disorganized. Since she came from a setting where the local clergy group was quite successful, she decided she could help get things going in her new community. Implementing her ideas required approaching male colleagues in other parishes, and Harriet did so with the assumption that collaboration would be possible. She knew that she had the experience and expertise to help. However, two years after starting this initiative, Harriet had gotten nowhere. Instead of finding her colleagues eager to collaborate, she found them either uninterested or actively thwarting her efforts.

Harriet fell into the trap of being better at a skill than a dominant male in her peer group. Women in leadership, in the church and out, quickly find that it is deadly to "do better" at any task than a dominant male, lest he be humiliated. Coger emphasizes that "a humiliated or resentful dominant does not make a supportive peer." She cites one male manager who comments, "It's OK for women to have these jobs as long as they don't go zooming by me."[17] Expressing no surprise at this comment by a man, one woman offers this caution: "The woman who does exactly as a man does, but does it better actually threatens the man. Even though she is succeeding, she is breaking down bridges and making enemies in the men's camp." Thus women commonly remind each other, "The better you do the worse it gets."

Susan Faludi sheds light on why female success may be so threatening to men. She points out that the single most significant indicator of masculinity, to men, is their role as providers for women.[18] If women are "doing better" than men, or are at the very least able to take care of themselves, thank you very much, their success is not just their success. It is a terrifying threat to men who will no longer feel like men when they are not in charge of taking care of women. Women don't understand this because, for them, gender identity and success are not related in the same way.

Success may also earn female leaders the wrath of other women who live by the white male paradigm. Because some women also believe in the white male system, they continue to think that the problems they experience are their own fault. Unconsciously, they direct anger internally, against themselves. When another woman does well, her success reinforces their own lack of self-esteem. In this dilemma, they have only two choices. First, project onto the other woman. Blame her for her success by saying it's wrong or deviant or unfeminine. If they don't do this, they have only one option left: direct more hatred against themselves by wondering: "If she can do so well, why can't I? The problem must be me. There *is* something wrong with me." Women not so bound by the white male paradigm will not have this problem.

Female leaders caught in this trap often find themselves "holding back" out of fear of retaliation or fear of visibility that might bring them criticism. In fact, Rosabeth Moss Kanter points out that "fear of success" in women may actually be in part fear of retaliation.[19] A recent psychological study of 229 young men and women supports this view. The study concludes that it does not help a woman to have men perceive her as competent. It further concludes that men are more likely to have their minds changed by a tentative, self-deprecating woman than by a woman who acts like she knows what she's talking about. Women, on the other hand, prefer self-assured women. Researcher Linda Carli concludes, "A woman who behaves in a high-status manner, i.e., a woman who is very direct and sure of herself is threatening to a man."[20]

Like Cinderella

These traps make working women into Cinderella, the poor sister who must work hard for little or no reward, and whose work is fundamentally devalued. Like Cinderella, the working woman can't get out of the trap by working harder or better, by making her male peers and superiors feel comfortable, or by doing a superlative job at her assigned tasks. What the working woman needs is the fairy god-mother to come and whisk away the old paradigm for one short evening, so that everyone around her can see the world in a new way. In this new world, her ways of working are valued differently, and the woman really does become a "new person" in the eyes of everyone around her. Of course, she is the same. It's the paradigm that has changed.

Chapter Eight

Harassment and Other Hazards

A woman's gender is most painfully a liability when her sexuality comes into play. When a women is regarded and expected to behave primarily as a sexual being, because she is a woman, she can easily be trapped in situations that violate her privacy, her physical boundaries, or her sense of self as whole. Harassment is the most widely discussed (though still poorly understood) trap women face in this respect. Others include "How Do I Look?" and "Be Yourself." Women often report feeling unsafe, ashamed, or exposed, because these traps are a part of their regular experience.

Harassment

At a recent clergy retreat, the participants divided into four groups for discussion, writing ideas on newsprint. When the groups came together, the retreat leader, a consultant, picked individuals to post the results. Two men were chosen from the first two groups. By the time that a petite woman rose to post the results from the third group, it was obvious to everyone in the room that she would not be able to reach high enough to post her papers with the other two. There was laughter and joking as the group watched her struggle. After she sat down and the fourth and final newsprint had been posted, the leader stopped the meeting and recounted to the group what he had just seen: The only time there had been joking and laughter during this exercise was when the woman stood to post her results. Furthermore, he observed, the men had laughed and the women had been silent.

**THEME EIGHT:
Women feel unsafe because their physical boundaries are routinely compromised.**

This incident is another example of loyalty testing. But it is more than that. Though men call it hazing, it is harassment, as much as loyalty testing is a form of harassment. It shows that sexual harassment isn't always about explicit sex. It can also be about how a woman (or a man) looks. What is so shocking about this example is that it was group harassment. And after the men were confronted with it, they were angry that they had been "set up." They expressed little concern for the woman who had been harassed. They accused the consultant of "ruining" their discussion.

We all know about harassment. We've read and heard about it and most of us have probably been to harassment workshops that are designed to teach us what is and isn't harassment. Presumably, then, we all know that sexual harassment in the workplace is forbidden. Nevertheless, it still happens routinely, and many forms of harassment are not well recognized. Sociologist Barbara Gutek suggests that harassment often still goes unrecognized because we—both men and women—tend to have a bias about sexual behavior as good, no matter what the context. The assumption, when employees see a sexual advance, is that both parties are wanting and enjoying it.[1] Nancy DiTomaso and Jeff Hearn add to this the observation from research that women tend not to name obvious harassing behaviors as discriminatory[2] until they reject subordinate occupations and begin to move into "men's jobs."

Harassment is wrong, demeaning, and shaming to women. Yet it remains one of the traps for women who work in the white male paradigm. "As long as it is culturally acceptable to treat women as sex objects, some sexual harassment is bound to occur."[3] It should not be forgotten, furthermore, that harassment is not just a power play. It is, by the harasser's choice, a sexual power play.[4] Paradoxically, it may also be unconscious, because the man—so steeped in the ways of the prevailing paradigm—sees his behavior as "the way a man relates to a woman."

One clergywoman recounts this encounter she had with a superior: "He had no clue about how to supervise women. So he just dealt with us as if we were his 'girls.' He didn't know, because not one of us ever said, 'Don't pat me on the butt; don't give me a bear hug when you see me in public; don't kiss me on the cheek and wish me a Merry Christmas.' And because these guys have done it for so long, when somebody calls them on it, they are clueless. And of course, they say they are innocent because as far as they know, they are. They didn't have any sexual intention, and no one ever said anything to them until allegations were made publicly. Part of me says we women have to take some responsibility for that. We have to tell them," she emphasizes.

Sexual harassment is defined by one denomination as "any sexually related behavior that is unwelcome, offensive, or fails to respect the rights of others."[5] Thus, unwelcome comments, touching, gestures, jokes, and the like are all included in the catalogue of harassment. I would include in this definition at least two behaviors that are not always identified as harassment. First, ridicule about a woman's size or body type, even if it is not sexually explicit, is harassment. The incident at the clergy retreat, related at the beginning of this chapter is an example.[6] Second, those situations in which a woman finds that her job opportunity, advancement, or leadership role is questioned or curtailed because she is considered to be primarily "domestic" constitute harassment. An example is provided by the woman who returned from maternity leave and was chided by her boss for not applying immediately for a promotion with the words, "What's the matter, don't you have enough energy for your job anymore?" In this case, the woman was explicitly accused of laziness because her new motherhood was taking too much energy. The criticism was leveled in a chiding and therefore unofficial way that is difficult to counter, and was not tied to any real evaluation of her job performance.

Men often commiserate with each other about the fact that, in a highly sensitive environment, "We can't even compliment a woman anymore, because she might charge harassment." It may be true, but it's not the fault of women. This is exactly the bind. Even if women are spared the experience of harassment, they are still held responsible for the fact that "we all have to be so careful." In a similar way, women are blamed for sexuality in the workplace at the same time that they are expected to be sex objects.

In fact, the problem is not women, it is a sexualized workplace that we view as neutral. Sex role stereotypes that are a part of the prevailing paradigm present women as sexual beings but continue to reinforce the view of men as organizational beings, no matter what they do. This fact, verified by research, leads Gutek and others to characterize the workplace as "an outgrowth of the male psyche."[7] When we view the workplace as neutral, we are caught in the prevailing paradigm and we will continue to hold women responsible for any manifestation of sexuality in the workplace. The way women look, the fact that they are "tempting to men," that they have babies and have to take time off, in the end the very fact that they are present in the workplace *as female*— all these realities are held against women when we operate out of the white male paradigm without the awareness that another worldview is possible. This is the essence of harassment.

In the church the ways in which women are singled out for being women take on theological overtones as well. Because of the church's prevailing dualism about sexuality and spirituality, "even to have women in leadership confronts the myth that identifies women with sexuality and body and men with spirit and intellect. Women are embodied pastors. They bring their sexuality with them." By office they are granted power to function as clergy, but as females they are traditionally denied access to the power of sacred masculinity that resides in ordination. Their very being calls into question old ways of thinking, and often the women themselves bear the pain of being rejected.[8] Says one clergywoman: "It's a strange thing, but it's almost like the men in that pastoral role can somehow be sexually neutered" but women cannot.

Because organizations are largely viewed as neutral even though they are in fact structured to reinforce notions of sexuality pleasing to men, women are in a real bind. "Although their attempt to manage their sexuality is a response to organizational structure, policies, or norms, they frequently have to deal with it on a personal level or treat it as an exclusively interpersonal encounter"[9] even though they know it is not. Thus they are in the bind that Pastor Ellen faced when she received inappropriate and suggestive comments from a colleague. What should she do? If she talked to him directly, she'd be treating the encounter as purely personal, and she knew it wasn't. She had heard from other women who had been harassed by this particular man. If she complained, she was taking a risk. He was powerful and well connected in the denomination's network. She decided to mention the incident to her bishop, just as information, not asking for any action to be taken. Several weeks later, Ellen's bishop summoned her to meet with the man in question. In the encounter Ellen's bishop treated the incident as "just something between you two that we have to work out." Ellen was distressed by the encounter, which was arranged without her permission. But she also knew that nothing else she could have done would have had better result. "Women always have to set the boundaries," advises one clergywoman, "and it's an absolute trap."

Barbara Gutek's studies show that the workplace is sexualized even though most people don't think it is and don't consider any sexual expression in the workplace appropriate. This leads her to wonder: is it possible to create a social setting in which sex is clearly inappropriate? She thinks not. The church, however, tries, and thus becomes a victim to the most perverse of all forms of sexual harassment: clergy sexual misconduct—the use of a relationship of trust between pastor and parishioner for sex. The instances of clergy misconduct are frighteningly high, and we wonder why. But it shouldn't be such a mystery. The church actually denies the sexuality of its male clergy in an effort to create a radically asexual environment. That which is denied emerges then in its darker forms, as "conduct unbecoming clergy." Should we be so surprised that so many men are victims? No, but we should be clear that in this tragedy for the church, men are most often the victims of the church's views of sexuality and women are victims of the inappropriate behavior of men.

How Do I Look?

Joellen, a well-known freelance professional, had decided it was time to take a job. She applied for a position for which she was well qualified. She knew her denomination was looking for women, and although she knew about the gender trap, she hoped this would help her receive careful consideration. Indeed, she was called back for a second interview. By this time, she knew that her main competition for the job was another woman—younger, less experienced, but better looking. Joellen knew the outcome even before she got the call. The younger, prettier woman got the job.

Women know that appearance counts. Anyone, male or female, in senior management knows this. "Dress for the job you want, not the job you have"—so goes the proverb. But for women, it counts in ways that it should not. Most often, being attractive helps. In many cases, being too attractive hurts. And sometimes being plain is an advantage. The point is that how a woman looks is always an issue. Appearance is never a neutral factor. This is because, as Schaef reminds us, in a white male system of thinking, everything and everyone is first and foremost defined sexually.[10] Women remind men of sex one way or another, depending on what they look like. Whether appearance helps or hurts a woman depends on standards set by men. Generally, more attractive women make men feel better. Thus appearance may help land them jobs. What Joellen didn't know is that after you've got the job, the tables are often turned. Pretty women "aren't supposed to be too aggressive." So, the woman who makes men feel most uncomfortable is usually the very attractive woman who is also very aggressive, direct, and competent. To a man, she looks most like a woman, but she acts least like one!

Sex roles are used to shape men and women's behavior in the workplace.[11] Among the characteristics of femaleness is "being a sex object," and "there is no strongly held comparable belief about men."[12] The gender dualism that results when male and female are separated and thought radically different "allows women to become objectified and commodified as objects to be used by the dominant males to whom they belong."[13] The carryover of these sex role stereotypes into the workplace is responsible for the view of women as sexual beings and men as organizational beings. Unfortunately for women, it seems one cannot be both, "because femaleness is viewed as not-maleness." Thus women's perceived sexuality can blot out all other characteristics of her as a worker.[14]

A strikingly attractive woman will have a particular problem being viewed as competent. Her looks are distracting to men. Dualistic thinking makes it difficult for her to be seen as competent because she is so attractive. And it's demeaning for her in the extreme to be reminded that her looks are what counts. Says one woman, "It is true that people who are more physically attractive probably get recognized or get jobs or whatever, but at the same time, there's something really degrading about somebody telling you that you have nice legs. I remember walking out of a presentation once and somebody said that. And here I had just done this incredibly brilliant presentation!" It was demeaning, she adds, but she was supposed to hear it as a compliment. "I really wanted to turn around and slug the guy," she says, adding, "Once again, it was up to the woman (me) to figure out how to deal with this with some integrity."

"Women still have to deal with what is the appropriate dress for a variety of occasions. It's one more thing that women have to think about," says another woman, adding, "but underneath . . . there is a very serious matter. I think it is important for women not to deny their sexuality because to some degree our energy comes from our sexuality and from our comfort with it."[15] Still, she added, women have to be very careful not to be misinterpreted, and "women who happen to be blessed with good looks have to be very careful not to present themselves in ways that might be interpreted as using their sexuality." Sheppard calls this the woman's task of "managing her gender." Gutek warns that women who don't manage it to the standards set by men will be blamed, even though it is the sexuality of the workplace, not the women themselves, which create the bind that women are in.

What is doubly troubling about a woman's inability to be both sexual and organizational at the same time is that women are not the ones choosing.[16] Men are the architects and guardians of the prevailing paradigm, and they do the choosing. As we have said in the previous section, the workplace is socially structured to meet a man's sexual need; therefore, men choose how women will be viewed. What's a woman to do? Either she takes on the assigned sexual role in her behavior and dress or she tries to cast it off by being asexual. If she chooses the latter, warns one clergywoman "the men say, 'Oh, she's a dyke.' "

Men, on the other hand, do not have any experience of being sexualized in the workplace. Gutek's studies uncovered startling examples of men's overtly sexual behavior that was not seen by coworkers as sexual at all, but "was subsumed under the stereotype of the organizational man"—merely part of being competitive, assertive, goal-oriented, even rational.[17] For this reason, men may reject outright the experience of women as sexual beings in the workplace, as did one man who read this chapter in manuscript form and became very angry. He simply could not believe that looks really are a factor for women in ways they are not for men.[18] By contrast, other men are to be commended for working very hard to break out of the prevailing paradigm, as did the denominational executive who told us, "Women are my colleagues. I see them doing good jobs and doing them well. They have become my friends, not my sex objects."

In the church, women experience a unique twist to the "How do I look?" trap. In this environment, there is significant advantage to being plain. Men working for the church carry a heavy load of guilt about sex and sexuality, because Christian piety values an asexual environment. Yet, because they are male system thinkers, they tend to define relationships sexually and they see women as sex objects. The men are in a real bind. They are reminded of sex by women, as all men are, but they feel guilty about it, perhaps more than the average man, because the church has taught them that sex is evil. For these men, it may be more comfortable to work with women who are plain, women who remind them less about sex. And so the women around them have to be plainer. Always, it's the women who must meet the sexuality standard set by men. That, too, is part of the prevailing paradigm.

Be Yourself

Elizabeth is typical of Judy Rosener's interactive leader. When making decisions, she places a high value on engaging the people on the denominational staff, which she leads. Yet, the department that includes this staff exists within a very hierarchical system. At the same time that Elizabeth works very hard to use interactive leadership, she is pressed by the hierarchy around her to be less interactive. It's a delicate balance, but Elizabeth has been encouraged by the staff and the many ways they appreciate her style. In fact, when she gets pressed for time and is pulled away from staff concerns, she often hears from the staff members that they want her to be more caring, attentive, and connected to their concerns and tasks. This request makes sense to Elizabeth, because it fits her leadership paradigm. Recently, however, the staff gave a different message. The department was facing a major decision, and Elizabeth set up a system that would engage people at all levels in setting direction. The staff responded by complaining that she was not decisive enough, that she didn't seem to know what she wanted to do, and that she was taking too long.

Women often get caught in the trap of being themselves. Of course, it is essential for women to lead from their own paradigm.[19] But whenever they do, there is the possibility that they will be considered weak or ineffective. When this happens, it's because the woman is leading from one paradigm and being judged by another. For women working in the white male paradigm, which values decisive, directive leadership, and action over process, there are many dangers to "being yourself." Asking for ideas can be interpreted as not having answers. Sharing information and power "allows for the possibility that people will reject or challenge the leader" or her authority. Generating enthusiasm in employees can be interpreted as cheerleading.[20]

Denominational bureaucracies may have more problem accepting a woman's style of leadership, and therefore "letting women be themselves," than parishes, in the view of many women. "Congregations find themselves served well" by shared leadership, "because one style of leadership fits one person and another style may fit another," says one church woman with many years of experience working in church organizations. "But, church organizations are not yet ready for partnership. They want a CEO. They want someone in charge. There are just some roles, sometimes it's the pastorate of a very large church, or the head of a denomination, or the head of an ecumenical agency, where the office is seen as an exercise of power that requires 'a man' to do the job. I've tried to the degree possible to build a team with my staff, but I think it's not easy when it's not constructed as a team and it's very clear that I'm in charge."

Women must decide to what extent they can use their own paradigm of leadership and to what extent they need to play by the rules of the prevailing paradigm. In this respect, their task is that of any minority group. Even though they may have unique ways of leading, they still must know the ways acceptable to white men, and to a certain extent, use them. This is true as long as the prevailing paradigm prevails! "Women have to know how white men think and what the white male culture is. Whether or not they buy into it, they have to know what it is. If you don't enter in knowing that, you absolutely can't be heard. And if you're always fighting against what is, you reduce your own ability to make something happen," one woman advises.

Knowing how men lead and learning to appreciate their paradigm and operate within it is not all bad for women, by their own admission. One woman puts it this way: "Men change women for the positive just as women change men." One way is in demonstrating how to use power effectively. "Women often are afraid of using power, and I think there's a certain amount of dishonesty about that because it's not as though we don't understand it." She adds, "Men help women be clear and come to grips with what it means to have a powerful job and use that power effectively."

For women, this learning must always take place in the context of being a woman. "Act like a man" is not the answer.[21] "Unisex ministry is hardly worth what it costs a woman to establish herself in what it is still fair to say is a man's world."[22] One longtime church woman has this advice for her younger sisters. "The secret of being a successful woman is to be a woman, to be comfortable being one, to dress like one, to act like one, to think like one, knowing that you may be doing that in a male world." Southern Baptist pastor Nancy Sehested agrees, reminding women that God has admonished us "to put new wine in new wineskins, so there will be life anew for all."[23]

Because they must work as immigrants in a foreign land, so to speak, women must also "have access to people with whom [they] can be real."[24] One woman pastor asks, "Where are we allowed to say what we want to say? I think this is a question women have had to ask in a different way than men. Men are able to say certain things and to be respected even if they are different. On the other hand, women tend to get silenced by the church when they express differing views."

Many women persist in being themselves even in the face of criticism, and often they win over their male critics. One volunteer who became the first woman on a very powerful board was greeted by a longtime male member with this comment: "I know I'm supposed to welcome you, but you know, we've gotten along for many years without a woman and I don't see why we would need one now." In the face of such a challenge, this woman persisted in being herself and serving with dedication in a style that suited her. A year later this same man said, "You have brought a dimension to this board that we have never had before. I want you to know that I am so glad you were the first."

Safety Hazards

Safety is the ultimate issue for women where these traps are concerned. Women are physically threatened by harassment. It renders them uncertain about their physical well-being. Because harassment can happen anytime, even in the places that should be safest, women feel vulnerable most of the time. Women are also physically threatened by the constant focus on their appearance. Appearance shows; it's available for men to comment about all the time. Living with a body that is routinely violated by talk and by inappropriate action is a source of vulnerability that men cannot understand unless they feel it. One woman pulls no punches in saying: "Only men who have been in prison can appreciate what it is like to be in constant fear of bodily invasion." Women live with it, indeed, have little or no experience of being physically safe. In the face of this kind of challenge, it is a courageous woman indeed who chooses to be herself.

— — Chapter Nine — —

Traps
for Men

Men have plenty to say about the traps women negotiate on a daily basis in the male world of the church. The basic message is clear: "We are trapped too." Sometimes the traps are the same for men; more often they are different. Always, they are related in some way to men's dominant position in the prevailing paradigm. Because men are all members of the dominant club, they are hindered by stereotypes of women and by the very behaviors for which they might be rewarded in an all-male workplace—principally their tendency to be action-oriented. On the other hand, much like women, they are trapped by the hierarchical system and by stereotypes of them and what they are supposed to be like. Finally, positioned as dominants, men must always fear losing that position—and all the power that comes with it, even if the small number of coveted positions in the top ranks of their district or denomination make it unlikely that they will ever get that power.

Stereotypes Die Hard

"We have to start with the stereotypes we carry around," says one pastor. "In the male-dominated workplace, they get shared and discussed, but in the end, we each have our own that we must confront and deal with." They are like the demons that don't go away. "We are confronted by the presence of women in the church," says another pastor, "and we must ask ourselves, 'How do I look at this person now?' This is a brand new deal."

These stereotypes may include the belief that women are (1) not as skilled as men, (2) not as capable of critical thinking, (3) too emotional, (4) too willing to make decisions on the basis of personal experience rather than objective analysis, (5) less dedicated to their careers, (6) indecisive, unable or unwilling to make tough decisions, and (7) not as good at the financial aspects of leadership.

In order to overcome the stereotypes, we must not only know how women are different, "we have to value those differences," says another pastor. This means not getting caught in the trap of dualistic think-ing—assuming that because we are different, we are better than women, or that women think they are better than us.

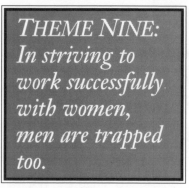

THEME NINE: In striving to work successfully with women, men are trapped too.

Many of us "have grown up with the idea that, by and large, men are superior in creative leadership and administration," one churchman ad-mits candidly. "Men have not seen women in a leadership role long enough," another adds. "They just have not been conditioned to realize that women can do these jobs better than a lot of the men we might have on the list." That's stereotyping. And "the real conflict comes when women are doing the same job as men, and the men refuse to value them," another concludes. To the extent that we have been influenced by this view, he adds, we have to overcome this assumption of superiority, in spite of the fact that most of the culture around us still tells us we are superior.

This trap is tricky and tempting for men. Theology contributes. "A man who is a pastor or leader in the church may see himself as doing the will of the Lord. Many people have told him that—our theology tells him that. And he feels called to do that." It is very tempting for a man to assume, furthermore, that only he can do it. Theology has told men that too, and in this all-important respect, theology contributes to gender stereotyping.

Hierarchy: Buying In or Opting Out?

Men generally appreciate the contributions that women make to leadership, particularly their ability to relate well to people and to bring more collaboration to the decision-making process. Says one pastor: "I do think that women are more conscious [than men] of the need to nurture people and involve people in decision making. When women do take the nurturing approach, they bring a caring to the workplace, much more sensitivity toward the person than men have been taught. We men come too much out of the pyramid style of leadership." Another offered this comment about a senior woman with whom he works: "She is both an effective manager and a person who has modeled caring in her life wherever she has been. She is, overall, a better administrator than the [male] leader of our [office]." These men agree that they can learn from women in leadership.

Men also want women to be treated fairly. "I want to start with fairness," one pastor emphasizes. "I don't think there should be job discrimination in the denominations, and I do think there should be equal opportunity for women." But for this pastor, and for other churchmen, the denominational hierarchy gets in the way. This is the first way that the prevailing paradigm is a trap for men.

"The tough part of being an administrator is rising above the institutional limitations in dealing fairly with women," says one pastor-administrator. And so in the end, "the most serious threat in the limiting environment of hierarchy is that we won't hire the right person for each job—woman or man." His point: when we aren't free to hire women without questions, we aren't really free to hire men either. Everyone gets caught in the employment trap because we still have limitations about hiring women. These limitations may be masked as opportunities, as in the directive to "hire a woman for this job." Neither men nor women like this. It's demeaning to everyone's professionalism. On the other hand, women and men agree that it is important to be intentional about placing women in leadership positions. It's a real dilemma. Men tend to get caught in this trap frequently, because they are still more likely (than women) to be in the position of doing the hiring.

A second way in which the prevailing paradigm of hierarchy traps men is by blinding them to the possibility that a different style of leadership might be possible or even preferable. Though collaborative leadership models have been around for as long as twenty years, they have not necessarily had much influence in the denominations. Thus, the prevailing view in the churches that hierarchy is still necessary. One denominational administrator puts it bluntly: "The real world of decision making is still hierarchical."[1] Women or men with a more collaborative style, he says, have moved up in the denominations not because they are gaining more power there but because the church is losing power in the culture. "I am cynical enough to think that if the churches had the power they had in the 1940s and 50s, they would still have a lot more of the persuasive and even dogmatic power people, male or female, in top positions." The power positions in any organization are going to stay with the ruthless, male or female, he believes. Most of these leaders happen to be male.

This creates a lose-lose dilemma for men. On the one hand they can learn to be more collaborative and lose out on the power positions. On the other hand, they can continue to be hierarchical in their style and be labeled "jerks" by their new female peers. The only way for men to get out of this dilemma, they say, is to see beyond the current hierarchical paradigm, to a vision of leadership that is no longer based on "I win; you lose," because "my power depends on your weakness."

But let us stay with the hierarchy long enough to pause and acknowledge what does happen to men who try to move beyond power games to collaboration with women and other men. As long as the white male paradigm based on hierarchy prevails, men who attempt to move beyond it encounter some of the same traps that women experience. They report feeling invisible, having their ideas ignored or taken over by more powerful men, or being judged ineffective.[2] A man who decides to move beyond hierarchy to collaboration in leadership is always fighting the cultural expectation that he should be decisive, "in charge," aloof, analytical, even domineering. When he is not, others around him may wonder "What's the matter with him?" or they may say, "He doesn't know how to be a leader." This is as much a trap for men as it is for women.

Fear of Change and Loss

Men are afraid, and their fear traps them. This may be the biggest trap of all. When I asked men what they fear, they could give me a list. They fear losing power, positioning, and the job itself. They fear opening up. They wonder if a different way will really be better. They don't know what women are really "up to," and they fear the lack of accountability that nonhierarchical leadership implies. They fear women's rage. They fear that women will really be better than they are at the job. And in the final analysis, they are so used to the way the game is now played that they suspect women are trying to "put one over on them" by pretending to be collaborative while they secretly steal the power.

Let's start with jobs, and the power and positioning that come with them in the denominations. "Being in the parish, as hectic and nutty as it can be, has with it an element of being taken care of, and there's a certain amount of power that goes along with that," one pastor confides. "All of these givens are shaken when the ground rules change or when the landscape changes and suddenly women are involved. It's not totally a man's work world anymore in the church." What this means for men is that they can't count on the church to be "a place where we can do our guy bonding," as one pastor puts it. More threatening still, the men don't get the jobs they could once count on. "White males over fifty have lots of cause to recognize that they are not going to have as much automatic opportunity to do things as their fathers did, and that's a realistic assessment," insists a layman.

Others affirm this view. "We have gone through a period of time where you could just about write yourself off if you were a white male, because you're not going to get the job," a denominational administrator observes. The same lament is heard from those men who have qualified themselves for seminary teaching positions. In fact, several of the men interviewed had lost out on coveted jobs at key points in their careers. They generally recognize, as one says, "that women have experienced this for centuries, so how can we complain?" Still, the loss is difficult to deal with when it is personal. Men have had to learn the hard way that "no one job is all that important." They report being angry and grieving. The discipline for them: "Finally being able to see that the woman who was hired brings something to the job that I could not, and saying to myself, 'That's OK. I'll go do my thing somewhere else.' " This point of reconciliation with the loss of a job is hard to achieve for men who feel that the woman hired was not as qualified as they themselves were. On the other hand, for those who were able to reconcile the loss, they went on to work successfully with women, in some cases the very women who got the jobs they sought. One pastor summarizes his experience succinctly: "I got over it and I am blessed by that."

But even where jobs are not lost, men fear that power is lost. One denominational administrator who turned over a major project to an all-female team found the men in the department were "very uncomfortable because they perceived that they were losing power." This fear comes from a principle of hierarchical thinking, the trap of viewing power as a limited commodity. It also mixes like a volatile chemical with men's other power losses, observes one pastor who points out candidly, "Many men in middle age notice a diminishing of power and vitality. It is all part of the loss of male potency. Power is lost not only to women who challenge. It is lost politically, financially, and in a number of ways. So there is a kind of built-in fear of the loss of power for men. I suppose that any new challenge, particularly if it is based on new rules, is even more threatening." Still, the fear of loss of power is based on the assumption that power is limited. This may be true for men biologically, but it is not necessarily true in the workplace if we can get out of the hierarchical paradigm.

Men also fear opening up. One pastor recalls meetings at which the women in his office wanted to have a time of sharing "where you lay yourself on the table" and "the men just want to do business." His point: "The men get turned off by the women who almost insist that we talk about our feelings and our hurts and so on. The men go away grumbling, saying it's a waste of time. The women carry it too far, even though it is a strength they bring to the workplace." Men recoil, he says, because they are uncomfortable. Again, it's about power. "Revealing too much means that I might be giving up some information or something that would infringe on my power or demonstrate my weakness," he adds. It's also about unfamiliar territory for men. "We know intellectually that people are emotional beings," explains another churchman who works in administration, "but we have learned to keep our emotions down. So we often don't deal with other people (or ourselves) as emotional beings. We expect logic." Says another pastor: "We don't talk about relationships and personal things because we are uncomfortable with touchy-feely topics." When a woman asks a man to do this, she pushes his panic button.

She may also be pushing his patience. Men report frustration and impatience with the process orientation many women bring to the workplace, a difference illustrated by the opening dialogue in chapter 3. It is also a factor in the finger pointing over the decline of denominational curriculum. For decades, while denied any other opportunity, church women have functioned as credentialed Christian educators. In recent years the decline of attendance in the Sunday schools of all denominations has been blamed, by men, in part on a paralyzing preoccupation with "educational process" and not enough focus on results or content. Some men are impatient over this loss of influence in the Sunday school, and they blame the educators (many of whom are women) or their process talk.

For many women, personal sharing is an important part of the process. But when women ask for relational sharing, men often believe that they are wasting time. Furthermore, they fear that a lengthy process will leave them wondering where the accountability lies. They simply don't know how "getting to know you" contributes to getting the work done. In the final analysis, men often wonder "where these women are going," and are not so sure they want to go that route to complete a project, build a budget, or do any of the other tasks of parish or denominational life.

A part of men's wondering about "where these women are going" is a real suspicion that women are being manipulative. "Men are not so much gatherers," one pastor in a denominational executive post explains. "When women get together in groups we tend not to understand. We think it's a strategy or a conspiracy. We wonder: 'Why are those women getting together? Are they trying to figure out how to bash us?' When our women's executive group gets together they are rightly asking, 'What are some ways we can penetrate this all-maleness?' 'What they're doing over there' is nothing more than being a support to each other. Men don't need to do this because we're already together by the very nature of the denominational structure. Still, when the women do it, we're suspicious." Men, in fact are so suspicious of their female colleagues gathering that women have a joke about how men view them: "One woman talking to a man is a good colleague. Two women talking together are excluding themselves. Three women talking together are fomenting a revolution."

A case study of this phenomenon can be found in the hard work done in one denomination making major decisions about the future of its theological schools. In a process of several years' duration, a special task force worked widely throughout the church gathering information, working with a female church executive and an all-male group of presidents of the seminaries. The process involved collecting information from many sources. The presidents assumed in the beginning "that we had a secret game plan and that we were just looking for reinforcement for it," the clergywoman executive recalls. "They kept after us: 'Just tell us the decision. We know you have already made a decision, and you're just manipulating us into agreeing with it,' " they said. It took this executive and the task force a long time to convince the presidents that they were really asking for collaboration. One female member of the task force recalls, "We tried to be collaborative. We invited the decision makers to be a part of making the decision, but they didn't quite believe what they were being asked to do. They kept thinking 'There is a hidden agenda.' "

Taking Charge or Taking Over?

Men learn to take charge in their lives and at work, to get things done, go where they want to go, and make decisions.[3] This is a good way to be and to work, they say. They do have a point. A layman, commenting about administrative staff meetings in the church-related business where he works illustrates: "Sometimes we do have to engage in the critical process and decisions have to be made. If bad ideas are not confronted in constructive ways by sympathetic colleagues in our business, the bad ideas can and do take down other parts of the business." He is right of course, and his comment points out the value of task orientation, an ability to make decisions and move ahead.

In relating to women, however, this skill is often a trap rather than an asset for men. Women say the men are taking over, not taking charge. A clergyman gives an example of how he got trapped, speaking to his secretary one day: "I was trying to be collaborative," he emphasizes. "We were talking about an issue she had. I immediately tried to solve the problem and she said to me, 'I didn't ask you to solve the thing. I can solve it for myself. I just wanted your comment on it.' I thought, 'Well, that's interesting!' "

This clergyman was just doing what he does well, and he got caught. He assumed that his proposed solution would be accepted gratefully by his secretary, and it wasn't! She wanted to solve her own problem.

Another lay administrator in a church setting sympathizes. "I'm sure this is one of my great failings. I see myself as a problem solver and whenever I see a problem I like to deal with it and solve it."

It can be very confusing for men to get blamed for taking action, when all of their experience has taught them it's good to be action-oriented problem solvers. But in fact, there are many ways that taking action can be a trap. Another example: the male senior pastor who undercuts the authority and position of a female associate by taking charge too much. When parishioners request the senior pastor for work that is supposed to be under the authority of the associate, and the senior pastor takes over as requested, he's doing much more harm than good. He may get the immediate task done and he may satisfy the parishioner. But he seriously damages his relationship with his female associate in the process, even though he may not have meant to at all.

Taking action becomes a trap whenever it limits a man's ability to work with a woman. If the man takes action too quickly, as did the pastors in the foregoing examples, he limits a woman's ability to think through and resolve her own issues. Women don't need to be helped. They need to learn how to help themselves. "Unless a man is doing something that I am not physically able to do myself, I don't want him to do it for me," one laywoman emphasizes. "If he wants to help me, he can listen to me, and help me think through how to solve my own problem. That's what we women need help with. But instead, he does it for me." That's the trap.

Taking action is also a trap for men in other ways. It contributes to their view that they are always right, limits their ability to learn the value of engaging in process, which so many women bring to the workplace, and damages their listening skills. "It may also fragment us," one clergyman observes. "I think we as men tend to focus on the specific things that need to be done at each moment, and work on that. Many women seem to keep a better perspective on the whole picture, the whole problem."

Another clergyman sees the take-charge attitude contributing to values struggles among his colleagues, especially those that tend toward workaholism. "Most men put jobs number one. Women put family first or make family and job equal. Now we have a whole generation of men who are saying that the family has got to be more important. These are values issues." They surely are. A man who puts family first must decide that "getting things done" isn't always most important. He must equally value "just being there."

The S Word

Men are also trapped by the way in which we all ignore the sexuality of the workplace.[4] We have seen in the foregoing chapters of part 2 how the sexuality of the workplace affects women. The traps for men are somewhat different, probably less compromising overall, but nevertheless tricky.

Men are set up to be aggressors and encouraged by many complex cultural influences to see women as sexual objects.[5] When women enter the workplace as colleagues, men are required to make a radical shift in behavior, if not also in thinking. They must treat women as coworkers at the same time that they receive many subliminal messages that encourage them to keep on seeing women primarily as sexual beings. It's a shift that many men are struggling to make. Now, in the rarefied atmosphere of sexual harassment charges and countercharges, the demand on men to figure this all out is backed up by legal threats.

We have discussed harassment and how it affects women. Men are both victims and unwitting perpetrators. First, of course, is the recognized fact that, as one clergyman says, "we men have also experienced sexual harassment at the hands of women." Men do encounter unwelcome comments, touching, gestures, jokes, teasing about their size or body type, and situations in which their job opportunity, advancement, or leadership role is questioned or curtailed because they refuse the sexual advances of women. Men do not report the same kind of physical vulnerability that women feel when they are harassed. But they do find harassment an uncomfortable and difficult situation to deal with. On the other hand, men are often befuddled by charges that they have been harassers. Remember the male supervisor profiled in the preceeding chapter, who patted his female staff on the rear, hugged them in public, and gave them a Christmas kiss. He didn't have any sexual intention, and no one ever said anything to him until allegations were made public. He felt trapped. From his point of view, he was trapped.

All of this is the obvious. There is yet another way in which men are trapped by the covert sexuality of the church which is much less obvious and much more damaging. Men—especially male clergy—are supposed to be as genderless as possible.[6] It is true that men are able to establish and maintain their identity in the workplace apart from their sexuality.[7] This is a tremendous advantage for them, one that women envy with good reason. In the church, however, it becomes a disadvantage. Men in church leadership are powerful, visible figures in an environment that is intensely uncomfortable with any sexuality. As such, they are not only expected to have an identity apart from their sexuality. They are encouraged to deny that sexuality is any part of their identity at all. Men are victimized by the suggestion—or even the requirement—that they deny their own sexual energy. When they are successful in denying that energy in its positive form, it becomes negative and emerges in unhealthy ways. Men do crazy (sexual) things, and women—or children—become their victims. Nowhere do I see any evidence that men who do these things are understood to be victims of the church's fear of sexuality. Instead they are blamed and ostracized for being caught in a no-win trap. Certainly I am not suggesting that what men do with negative sexual energy is right. I am suggesting that there are predictable reasons why we now have so many legal cases of sexual misconduct by men consuming the time and energy of every major denomination. Men take the blame for doing the dastardly deeds. Women often take the blame too, for raising the charges. But nowhere does the church take the blame for its centuries-old denial of the gift of male sexual energy.

Walking on Eggshells

Men say they are also walking on eggshells when they relate to women. Another image they use is walking in a minefield. They never know when they will step in the wrong place, and boom! They are describing the emotion trap. One pastor explains it like this: "My experience has taught me that it's much more personal to women. Whatever 'it' is, it's more personal—controversy, success, whatever. And criticism comes across to them as 'You don't care.' But I do care! I care deeply. I'm just not likely to have the overt emotional reaction they have. Whatever happens won't impact the way I behave in a work situation." He knows he's been caught in the emotion trap whenever he is accused of "not caring" or when he gets a tantrum or the silent treatment.

The silent treatment works like this, as one man describes it. "Suddenly I'm trapped. I know something is wrong. I did something.

I am in trouble for doing it. I am also in trouble for not knowing what it is. And I can't ask because I am supposed to know." When this happens, the clergyman explains, he knows he has reacted in a way that the woman working or living with him[8] judges "emotionally inappropriate" or insensitive.

Men admit that in many important ways, they do not know how women feel. It's probable then that they do react with insensitivity. It's a dilemma for them, which one pastor poses this way: "How do we understand, at a feeling level, what happens to women? I find women less willing to tell us unless they can do it in a safe place. How can we let them say it and how can I feel it?" Nevertheless, men caught in the emotion trap still wish for honest confrontation rather than the silent treatment, the tantrum, or the political diatribe, which they view as negative confrontation. "Trust is the key issue here," says another clergyman. "If there is trust between us, I would welcome the confrontation. We can work through it."

"Jerks" Forever?

In the final analysis, it all comes back to stereotypes. Women are not the only victims. A common stereotype of men is very much to the point: Men are jerks. No matter what they do, men seem caught in the trap of being labeled "jerks" by women. This is the ultimate trap for men, one they can't seem to get out of, no matter what they do.

"Men resent constantly being called jerks," one pastor/administrator comments. Just like any other stereotype, it's an unfair label. Certainly, when we consider what men in the church are doing to welcome women and learn to work with them, they don't always deserve it.

"To a certain degree, I think many of the men are trying very hard to behave in a [more] collaborative way, but it's not easy for them, and some of them just can't do it," one clergywoman observes. "It's destabilizing to them. Suddenly they are not defined the way they used to be, in terms of their role. They experience loss of control and power. To say that they are not suffering through it is not fair, because some of them really are trying hard."

Still, women remain skeptical of men and their intention and ability to change. Men often are jerks, they say. "Certainly some men are less hierarchical now. It used to be there wasn't anybody. There are more now and sometimes it's because they have met and worked with a woman and been persuaded to more openness, but I don't know . . . I've never had a male pastor say that he and I are a team, and I have worked for five," says one clergywoman. She continues also to have to deal with men's stereotypes about women and about who they as men think they are supposed to be. "They'll say 'I didn't let you do that because I was protecting you.' I have to remind them that I don't want to be protected. I have a lot more problems with men who try to protect me than those who don't."

Says another: "I think that even when men talk about a team, they still see themselves as the coach who makes the decisions." She adds, "Many of them can see the value of collaboration, they can see the value of women equally to men. But it's so easy for them to 'help the girls out.' Then they still know who's running the place. It's second nature to them."

Indeed, overcoming what's "second nature" to them is the task for men, insofar as working with women is concerned. For those who succeed, there are new rewards to replace the old. Men who can treat women as colleagues have a greater opportunity to engage in leadership that honors process as well as results. They can bring their feelings as well as their ideas to the workplace. They can finally let go of the imperative to know everything and become learners as well as experts. They will also have an important opportunity to help women learn how to use power, be more task-oriented, and embrace forceful ideas as well as forceful feelings. Most of all, they will have the opportunity to know women more fully as partners in the workplace. These are the gains of collaborative leadership for men.

Part Three

Leading
Together
in the
Church

Changing and Growing Together

When the angel of the Lord appeared to Zechariah to inform him that his wife Elizabeth would bear a son in her old age, Zechariah asked an impertinent question: "How will I know that this is so? For I am an old man, and my wife is getting on in years." The angel replied: "I am Gabriel. I stand in the presence of God, and I have been sent to speak to you and to bring you this good news. But now, because you did not believe my words, which will be fulfilled in their time, you will become mute, unable to speak, until the day these things occur" (Luke 1:18-20).

Some time later, Gabriel went on another mission to the girl Mary, with a similar message. She too would bear a son. Incredible as this was to her, Mary's reply was quite different than Zechariah's had been, once Gabriel explained to her "how this could be."

"Here am I, the servant of the Lord," she said, "let it be with me according to your word" (Luke 1).

Zechariah was skeptical. He questioned, rebutted, resisted. Mary was skeptical too, and frightened as well. She accepted, waited, pondered. This is an instructive story for both women and men as we approach working together in the church. It is particularly instructive for men, who bear primary responsibility for "doing the right thing" in order to make a place for women alongside them in the leadership of the denominations.

Men are in control of the workplace in both church and secular settings. Economic necessity and a desire for a fuller life have brought women into a workplace that was heretofore reserved largely for men. One pastor puts it this way: "Women feel the imbalance because it is in the men's sphere that money is made and power is felt. Coming into that sphere, women bump up against men's way of doing things. Men do not get forced into the women's sphere in the same way.[1] Men can have two reactions. Number one: 'Ain't it awful.' Number two: 'It's great that women are bringing these new ways of doing things into our sphere.'"

> THEME TEN: There are tasks for women and tasks for men. Men's tasks come first.

So long as the patriarchy prevails, white men are still very much in control in the workplace. They have the power and the influence. They make—and therefore know—the rules of the culture. Primary responsibility for change belongs with them. Much is required of men in bringing about a better work environment in the church, for both women and men. The tasks are also difficult, including as they do both action and reflection. The active tasks of becoming educated, working daily with women, rethinking theology, changing language, and trying out other approaches to leadership are difficult enough, requiring men to give up their privileged status, admit sexism, and assist women to achieve positions of leadership alongside them. They must do this despite their fears.

"It's not totally a man's world anymore, in the church," one clergyman observes. "Men fear having power taken from them, being seen in a different way than they used to be seen." They also fear sharing themselves.

"We are less willing to open up. We don't have the relational skills that women have," another comments. "We aren't as willing to be brothers as women are to be sisters." Men, who are skeptical of collaboration with each other because they learn to be competitive above all things, are now required to create a shared work environment with women, whom they often see as the enemy, "taking away" their jobs and changing the rules. It will be difficult. They will feel the pain. They already do.

What men must do will require change on their part. Many of them have said that the example of a strong female figure early in life has helped them see beyond the threats that women pose to the possibility of working together. We shall hear more about this later in this part. In addition, men are aided by their training to take action, solve a problem, get something done. Action will be difficult, but not impossible. The harder tasks will be reflective.

Reflection comes first, agree both church women and men. Men must ask, then, how to reflect? In searching for an answer, they can look to both Mary and Zechariah. Mary accepted. She simply says, "OK, God, if that's the way it's going to be, let's see what happens (to me) next." This would be a good stance for men to take. It's risky of their positioning, to be sure. It was risky for Mary too. She could have been stoned.

Zechariah had some assistance from Gabriel in reaching a point of acceptance. Gabriel took away his voice, so that Zechariah could not protest. There wasn't anything else he could do, so he too had to accept the inevitable. And there is nothing quite so inevitable as a pending birth. Only once the birth had been accomplished and Zechariah had named the child according to God's plan, was he given a voice of his own again.

Women have tasks too. Theirs center around the issue of power. Women have more difficulty than men in coming to terms with power. We are ambivalent about it. We have trouble knowing and accepting our own, because we often can't distinguish between healthy, productive power and abusive power. Unfortunately, what we've often experienced in our lives is the abuse of power. We women have to claim our own power and move ahead. Once powerful we will have authority that is based on our own uniquely female experience. We will have "the ability to control ourselves, to establish our own criteria, and to rid ourselves of fear." This is a woman's authority.[2]

I do not mean to understate women's task or to put all the responsibility for change onto the backs of men. I do want to emphasize that unless men do their part, women's contribution will be of little account.

That's always the way it is for the dominant group. They bear major responsibility for change. The only other way is revolution.

Both women and men agree with this division of responsibility, as it were. Men have shown this, typically, by their action. Many individual men have stepped out and taken action that brings women into leadership in their denominations. Action is the witness of men, and it is here duly noted. They have worked to get women elected to top administrative posts; advocated for inclusive language; worked with women as peers in the parish; promoted women; gone to workshops to learn about how women work, think, and feel; graciously stepped aside when the job they wanted was given to a woman; called women to their parishes, and a host of other things. They have done all these things because, says one clergyman, "Many of us believe the traditional interpretation of male-female roles. The equality taught in the scriptures has been skewed (in the hierarchy) and needs to be corrected." Other men have advocated for women for exactly the opposite reason: because they consider the traditional inequality still taught by their denominations to be wrong. All the men who take such action on behalf of women are demonstrating that they are willing to move beyond life in the white male system.[3]

Women confirm that men have the responsibility to take such action. "We are here," says one clergywoman. Women are here to stay in the denominations, as pastors, as lay professionals, and as volunteers. They will not go away. By their presence, which is often accomplished at great personal cost, they provide impetus for change. The presence of women is a demand—on men and on systems—to change. Apart from dealing with their ambivalence about power and carving out their own styles of leadership, maintaining a presence is the principal task of women.

— — Chapter Ten — —

What Men Must Do

Men can do much to further the cause of women in church leadership, so long as they start out as listeners rather than brokers. The first steps for men should be reflective—a looking inward to themselves, and then a period of deeply listening to women. After this has been done, men can take action, by doing many things to assist women.

Admitting Sexism

The first step for men in understanding and accepting women in leadership is exploding the myth of the white male system. Men particularly must accept that this system is not an eternal reality, as if mandated by some natural order or hierarchy of domination. It is only a system. It is not innately superior to any other system. It is not omnipotent. It does not make men (or anyone) completely logical, rational, and objective.[1] Though many women are pessimistic about the ability of men to break out of the white male system, it is the essential first step,[2] and many men take on the challenge admirably. In fact, it is a very courageous man who outlines this recipe for change: "Every man must admit to himself that, at some level, he is sexist. Only then does he have the openness to learn and value a new system." In order to do this, men must hear the statement not as an accusation, but as a statement of fact. "I think we realize that we are sexist," an almost-retirement-aged layman adds candidly. "We will probably never cure ourselves, guys my age, of being sexist, but we have to deal with that. We have to work at it." It must become "part of our self-understanding," another suggests. Men are sexist because they all grew up in and benefited from the white male system. They can't avoid it. As long as they fail to accept this fact, they will be unable to break into a new paradigm. "I really believe that [the men] have to start dealing with the 'isms.' It's painful for all of us. It's not easy for white people to see that this is a racist society. It's not easy for men to see that this is a sexist society, but that doesn't mean that we don't deal with it," says one churchwoman.

Sexism is subtle and insidious. It causes the most damage when coming from the man who thinks he's not sexist. It's hard to get the issues on the table when there is denial or a masking of power at work. A lot of men in this category believe that women ought to be present in the leadership of the church, "but very few of them think we need equal numbers of women," says one clergywoman. "I don't believe that they really believe we would be better off if, for instance, half of the bishops were women or half of the seminary professors were women. I do not think that very many men think we would be better off if it were half and half." This is the essence of sexism, especially when it concedes that the culture does not want women to be equal. "These are the guys who are thinking how glad they are that we [women] are here in leadership, but they are still always watching to see if we measure up," a clergywoman observes. These are also the men "whose language may be totally, absolutely nonsexist, but whose way of operating is very sexist," and who "believe they can speak for women almost as well as women can speak for women." This is just plain dangerous, women say.

It's also important to recognize that men are not the only ones who have been duped by the white male system. Women have bought into the system too. That fact is remarkably well illustrated by the debate that still rages on the pages of management journals about whether men and women are, in fact, different in their leadership styles. These are the managers who think we are basically alike. The system is fine—people just need to adjust. Of course, not all women are collaborative leaders; not all men use the dominant male style.[3] This does not change the fact that all of us are in some way influenced by and biased by a system of thinking and behaving that is so pervasive in our personalities and cultural expectations as to seem the equivalent of ultimate reality.

Once we have gotten this far, it is instructive to observe how male leaders in the church react to the news that sexism is alive and well, and they themselves are nurturing it. They seem to fall into three groups.[4] First, there are the men who do not understand it at all. These are the men who can participate in a sexist behavior and not even recognize it, even when they are confronted with it. They are not callous or dumb, however. They simply cannot, under any circumstance, "get out of" the white male system or in any sense view the world apart from it. It is therefore impossible for them to imagine anything else. I do not know of any women in this group. Even if they deny it, women have experience at some level that helps them at least to see the white male system for what it is—a system with flaws like any other.

A second group of men react swiftly and decisively. These are men who react to the sexism of the white male system in classic white male style. "It gets in their face. They are willing to fix it, but it's like killing snakes," as one clergyman describes it. "You just get it out of the way and then you go on." They want to sit down with women, "hear all about it" and fix it. Do something. Do it now. Go on to something else. They are still shrouded by the white male system, though they see its flaws. The giveaway is that they approach "fixing the system" in typical male dominant style. It's a task to be accomplished and nothing more. Once it's done, we'll all go back to business as usual.

A third group of men display real courage. Almost immediately upon hearing about sexism or being confronted by their participation in it, they pause and listen. They do not do anything else. Above all, they do not claim to be feminist and they do not try to solve anything. They have some awareness that any activity they might undertake would cast them back into their own system. Thus, the very act of pausing is a "first move" away from the system. It is an act alien to the white male system's way of doing things, and it takes great courage and determination for a man to make this move. It is the beginning of real change. And though it is true that both men and women must undergo intense personal change in order to reach a point of working together better, it is necessary particularly for men to make this shift. They, after all, are the guardians of the white male system.

Men are beginning to speak up about facing up to sexism. One candid and personal account comes from the corporate executive who, after thirty years in the white male system, emerged in an organization run primarily by women. Of his past he recalls that "corporate culture is really white male culture. Men had the power, so we made the rules to suit ourselves. . . . Men have noticed that women don't seem to conform to all of our rules. But until very recently, most men never stopped to consider why. In fact we really didn't care much why. The corporate structure worked for men. If women wanted in, let them figure out how to make it work for them." He goes on to say that, despite his gradual metamorphosis, "most men in corporate America still don't know how to deal with women." Then he adds, "Please give us a hand."[5] Men in church leadership are in much the same situation, and many of them are asking for assistance in the same way. One clergyman now working in a denominational office with a large staff has told the women, "I know I am a man who was raised in a male system. You will serve me best by telling me when you think I am speaking or acting in ways that are inappropriate."

Openness to this kind of change, and in receiving help from women in changing, comes only to men who are willing to look inward. "Myself—that is the only one I can ever change," one layman says. It has been his greatest learning in regard to working with women. This inward looking paradoxically frees men "to see that women bring gifts to leadership that most men tend not to have," a clergyman observes. And that's what women ask for. "Assume from the beginning that we know what we are talking about, that we know what we are capable of doing," a laywoman asks. To do this, men must move beyond sexism.

Listen and Listen Again

It takes a lot of listening. This is what women want most. Over and over again in interviews women asked that men begin by listening. "We want a place at the table," says one laywoman, a professional in the service of her denomination. "Men cannot know what we want and what the possibilities are unless they listen."

Men may wonder why all the fuss, why the hue and cry about listening? "What women long for is to be heard," a female bishop replies. "The biggest shock for me, when I became a bishop, was that people actually listened and responded when I said something. I shared this observation with some of the other [male] bishops, and they didn't even know what I was talking about. I decided that male pastors and male bishops are used to being listened to. They take it for granted."

"Men have to listen almost as enemies. They can pretend they are allies. They can pretend they are sympathetic, but it is very dangerous. They have to listen as aliens—or as if we are aliens. They can't pretend to know, because a lot of times they don't know," one laywoman cautions. This is the challenge to men. "They need to hear our experience as valid, not as deviant," another clergywoman explains. "It's going to be hard for them. In a way, women are at an advantage when listening is required. We already know their world and their way of doing things. We have to. But they don't know us very well," she explains.

Men agree. "We men have to accept the truth, whether we do it grudgingly or not," a church administrator admits. This is often difficult, especially when men are forced to listen in seminar settings. "We approach this often by grumbling, saying, 'Are they going to beat on us for another two days?' And after it's over, we say, 'They did beat on us for two days, but of course they are right.' And that sinks in. We are not dumb or insensitive. Most of us are men of good will. We are willing to learn and grow."

THEME ELEVEN: Women want men to listen.

A thoughtful and courageous clergyman has written about his own experience attending a conference for women clergy, in which the women discussed their leadership and participation in the church. Afterwards he wrote, "How can I describe how threatened I felt as a white American male clergyman when I found myself as the 'minority,' the outsider, the only representative of those who have caused these women so much pain and anger? . . . How can I describe my sadness as I listened to their stories, really 'hearing' and feeling for the first time the suffering inflicted on women in the male-dominated patriarchal church? . . . How can I describe the humiliation I feel when I realize that hardly any of my brother ministers have given even a passing thought to this pain, which we have inflicted on so many others?"[6] This is the essence of listening. It brings men to painful questions and opens them to a new way.

Listening can be the beginning of real change, men say, creating for them an opportunity to become aware of women apart from their male biases. If they can really hear women, they begin to see women differently. What they find out is surprising and often sobering. "I had no idea how much [sexism] hurt women. I had no idea how much pain is there. I just never thought about it," one administrator recalls. "I decided, well, I'm not going to contribute more of that [pain]. If I can, I am going to do something about it." A clergyman reflects on this realization with a question: "How do we [men] understand at a feeling level what happens to women?" He adds, "I find women less willing to comment on this unless they can do it in a safe place. How can we let them say it and how can I feel it?"

Particularly memorable for men has been their participation in a workshop on violence against women. The workshop, titled "Men Working with Women to End Violence Against Women,"[7] is offered for male leaders. Over a three-day period that is carefully programmed, men learn what it feels like to be physically vulnerable. Women observe the men as they become aware. Men report going to this event thinking they "already know," what women experience, and coming back stunned and deeply affected. "I didn't understand how I as a man bought into a system that oppresses women," recalled one African American clergyman after his participation in the event. Another comments: "I was impressed with the degree of vulnerability that women have to live with. . . . Women have reason to be fearful of how the men in their lives treat them, in terms of physical abuse as well as general manipulation." Another adds, "I was surprised by the number of incidents of violence that men confessed to having witnessed, having endured, or having perpetrated."[8]

Speaking from another denomination and another experience of the same event, clergyman Bruce Burnham observes: "Through interacting with those whose experience of discrimination has been real, through hearing the fear, pain, and anger in their voices, I have begun to change who I am so that I am more conscious of 'riding the wave of privilege.' This change has come only against great internal personal resistance and also against resistance from others [both men and women] who don't like to share this part of my life's journey because of the challenges to which it calls them."[9]

Mothers and Other Influences on Men

Though the admonition to listen is a demand that women make, it is also an invitation to men. "Very pragmatically, men need to listen as much as they talk. They need to follow as much as they lead. They need to have as much heart and emotion as they have head," a female professor says. "I think they need to be encouraged to feel safe enough to develop all of who they are. There are important contributions they can make that could be so wonderful if they could relax and be authentic." Men have something to gain by listening. They can learn "that women are capable of doing things and in most instances we are not to be feared," another churchwoman adds.

The result is often a change in men. Men who listen deeply begin to see women in a new way. They are able to accept the inevitable change that diversity implies. They are willing to use power collaboratively, to ask for help, to make the coffee at work, to scrub toilets and do dishes at home. Ultimately, these men are willing to change themselves. They become credible partners and mentors for women.

A man's readiness for such listening to women and acceptance of women depends on many factors. Churchmen say the most important influence has been their mothers or other strong women in their childhood. This may be because "mothers are practically the only experience people have with female power."[10] Or, it may be as Robert Bly and others have said, that men have no real relationship with their fathers. Our concern is not the reason why but the benefit derived. I was unprepared for how quickly and consistently men responded to

> *THEME TWELVE: Childhood experience teaches men how to work with women.*

the question: "What prepared you to work successfully with women?" They all said the same thing, without hesitation. These men remember mothers who were college educated, leaders in civic organizations or the church, or employed in business or other professional positions. Unusual in the early twentieth century, these mothers apparently not only led fulfilling lives themselves but also raised sons who never doubted that women are capable as leaders.[11] "This was part of the context I grew up in," one clergyman remembers. "I think I gained an openness for women to be in pretty important roles." Another adds: "I didn't realize until I got to college that not all women had the background my mother and grandmother had. Without anybody trying to impress me, I was very grateful for the very significant role women have played in my early life." This layman, now retired from a long career working for the church, reflects, "To the extent that I grew up in a household where women were often in charge, it is not difficult for me to trust women."

Women agree, with thanks to the mothers who have raised their sons this way. "I really see a difference in the families where mothers work or take volunteer leadership seriously," one female administrator says. "The men are much more respectful of women and they know how to do things themselves. They don't need to be carried. I can almost handpick the men who had moms who worked or who now have wives who work." Another churchwoman speculates that this is the reason many younger men are more comfortable working with women. "They have seen their mothers work; or they have seen their mothers in volunteer leadership, so it isn't a horrible thing when they have to work with a woman."

For men who have not grown up with boyhood experience of strong, capable women, there are other influences that contribute to their ability to work with women.[12] Often these are life-changing experiences that shake a man's assumptions about life and his place in it: divorce, death of a parent or spouse, or "something else that shakes us out of our unexamined assumptions," one clergyman suggests. "Different people need different things . . . but for a lot of men something like this has to happen. I don't know anyone who's simply gotten up on a Thursday morning and said, 'I'm pretty clear today. I've got a few hours. Let's tackle myself.' Something has to happen, something to force us."

For some men that "something" has been women who have confronted them about their style or their behavior in a particular setting, loss of an important job, or other events. For all of them, whatever the precipitating event was, it was in their word, "devastating," causing them to reexamine their assumptions about themselves, their work, the women around them, and the church. "They have to begin by reexamining their roles," a churchwoman reflects. "Something has to get them started."

Taking Action

Once men have undertaken the reflective tasks of looking inward and listening to women, they are in a position to take positive action. There are many things men can then do.

Create an environment of safety for women. Men cannot listen to women if women will not speak frankly. Women, who are not fools, will not speak unless "the coast is clear." Men help to create a safe environment when they are aware of and challenge the rules of the white male system. "I think women are expecting us men to create a safer environment, and they are right," one clergyman emphasizes. "I think women expect men to provide that, and I think we men feel that we should provide it." He adds that women are doing their part too. "The women's movement in our church hasn't been belligerent against men, but has been creatively working to get into dialogue with men."

Share power. This requires a different attitude about power and a willingness to share power with other men and women. Men must view power as abundant rather than limited in order to do this. They must embrace an empowerment model, "which means that if we share the power, we all have more," one laywoman explains. "If men could relax a bit and not be so fearful of what they are losing, it would help a lot," a clergywoman adds. "Short of that, trying out some collaborative decision making would be a step in the right direction." A new view of power requires men (or allows them, depending on one's viewpoint) "to be vulnerable and honest with each other," says one churchman.

Create an atmosphere of acceptance of women. As leaders themselves, men can set the tone by "having women in positions of leadership," says one churchwoman who is now a bishop in her denomination. She is aware that the environment of acceptance created by her male predecessor was a critical factor in her own election. Women will struggle to break the glass ceiling until men help them by preparing the way. This means several things for men. First, they must help women be better understood within the patriarchy. Second, they must help that patriarchy welcome change as women enter the church workplace. Third, they must, as individuals, continue to speak as men who personally believe in the value of women in the workplace.

Advocate for women in leadership. Men know that they must play an active role in getting women elected or appointed to leadership positions. Several talked about their participation in such efforts. Many had to take on the election rules of their denomination in order to get women elected as leaders. All had to overcome the barriers of habit that most often ensure that men get appointed or elected first. "In our denomination, if a man ran against a woman, the woman always lost," one clergyman recalls. He and other women and men, working together, devised a system of submitting a single nominee after a polling of delegates. It's a strategy that has worked to ensure that women and men share leadership roles. Until men get this aggressive about having women in leadership, we will be stuck with less desirable alternatives of which the quota system is one.

Advocating for women in leadership is an important role for men to play in the placement of clergy as well. "It takes serious advocacy to make sure that we put a woman on every search list," says one clergywoman who works as a bishop's assistant. "People need to be exposed to women clergy . . . to experience interviewing a woman so they'll realize we are normal human beings. Sure we can be ordained, but what difference does that make if we can't get hired?" One clergywoman, upon finding out that her bishop allowed a congregation to refuse to interview her just because she was female, said, "Isn't that the bishop's job? That's the kind of thing the bishop ought to be very objective about, and not let congregations do."

Affirm what women do. "We'd like the men to share the praise and credit," says one churchwoman. Women have to work twice as hard to get half as far as their male peers. There are many influences in the work environment that tell women they don't fit in or they don't do things the accepted way. When women do excellent work, they need to be recognized. Too often, their effort is taken for granted.

Notice things that count for women, even though they may not count for men. One clergyman recounts a discussion in his denominational office about elimination of part-time staff to save money. "I realized, even as we were discussing it, that all of our part-timers were married women. I don't think any of the other men in the room realized what was happening." This man did. They were contemplating a move that would affect the women on staff, but not the men. Instead, he said, "I asked the women part-timers to talk to the staff about being part-timers." With new information, the staff no longer saw cutting the part-timers as a fiscally sound solution. They found other ways to cut spending. This clergyman used his authority to raise awareness as well as solve the budget problem.

Don't label family concessions of the workplace "women's concerns." Family leave is of course mandatory now, legislated by the government. In some settings, employers are also providing flextime, day care, lounges for nursing mothers who work, and other benefits. Too often these are seen as "women's benefits." The concerns they address—for free time at home, for quality child care, and for infant nutrition—are also seen as "women's concerns." This kind of thinking is based on the unexamined assumption that the welfare of the family is a woman's issue. The welfare of the family is, in fact, an issue for women and men, and for the church. Every benefit the workplace provides for the nurturing of children and others in the family, regardless of who uses the benefit, is a concern for men too. Even a lounge for nursing mothers at work is a benefit for men as well as women because it assists in nurturing their children.

Men, of course, can and do use some of these benefits themselves. "Some of the things that people thought were put in place for women, like flextime, men find they like. The men are taking advantage of it," a laywoman in church administration points out. "The men say it's great. They can leave early to pick up their kids—and come in early the next day." It actually encourages their participation in family life.

Help women advance. This means ensuring that women are interviewed for calls, especially for senior pastorates and senior level lay positions. Women have not yet broken this barrier to their advancement. So long as the patriarchy reigns, women will not break this barrier without the help of men, primarily male bishops or other church officials who are responsible for the placement of clergy. This is important for men too. "Men need women to look up to," one churchman points out. "I think it is vitally important to have women bishops, to have women in positions that men look up to."

Mentor women. "Whether you are a man or a woman, someone has got to show you the ropes," says one churchwoman. For women emerging as leaders in a patriarchy, mentors must include men who know the system. One young woman tells of her intentional search for a male mentor. She picked a man who did not view leadership in a hierarchical way. He could, therefore, appreciate her style. At the same time, he could help her understand other men better. That's one thing male mentors do for women; another is provide women access to experience. A clergywoman tells of her mentors, men who "gave me the freedom to do what I could do well" and then taught her to do more. Her mentors helped her get more experience by "taking her in" to leadership situations she might not otherwise have had access to.

Women agree that they need men to mentor them into the white male system. "I was very fortunate to know some men willing to share with me and to be mentors to me—and to be men who were at the same time respectful of the fact that I am a woman," recalls one churchwoman. They weren't going to make me into a male leader. They just shared information with me, and then I could do with it whatever I wanted."

Preach. This is particularly a task for clergymen in senior level positions or for male bishops. One clergywoman who "just assumed" that the men in her cluster knew enough not to portray the woman at the well as "a fallen woman"—or Mary Magdalene as a prostitute or Bathsheba as the seducer of King David—found out she was wrong. "They need to be preaching about these texts that have been portrayed so inaccurately for so long," she says. Women can and will do this preaching, but men need to do it as well.

Include women in decision making. Of course this means having women on governing boards, and other decision-making bodies. It also means paying attention to how decisions are made—and by whom—on those boards as well as in the workplace. Just because women are present in leadership positions in the church does not mean that they are included when real decisions are made. Remember the female church leader who said, "So often [women] find out that the real discussions have happened somewhere else." Recall also the clergy-woman who said that in seven years of service to her denominational office, she had never been asked to participate in a major decision. And finally, remember the concern that women have about men who think they can speak for women.

Including women in decision making is particularly a need in those denominations that restrict the leadership roles women can hold. In these environments it may not be assumed that women should serve on boards or in advisory or staff capacities. When women are restricted from these roles as well as from the clergy, they do not have much access to decision making. If women in conservative denominations were allowed to participate in decision making, each woman would "bring her unique set of insights and wisdom to bear on issues in ways that could profit the team and the work."[13]

Insist that other men begin their change process as well. Men who deeply listen to women become sensitive to women's leadership concerns. They also become sensitive to the lack of awareness of their male colleagues. Remember the administrator who was surprised by the response of his male staff members when he turned a publication project over to the women. He was surprised because he was not threatened and the other men were. His firm resolve to allow the women to continue the project forced other men to take stock. That's what is required. Other men also talk about disappointment with their male colleagues. "They think they are young and hip. I think they are just full of male belligerence," says one clergyman of his peers. These men are both in a position to challenge and help their male colleagues to change.

Men's Choice

Men still have a choice about these matters; they are still in charge. The patriarchy is strong. Men can help women in leadership or not, as they wish. Women are here to stay, however. Change is afoot. Even if they choose not to assist women, men "still have to adjust, because it's not what it used to be," a clergywoman advises. This is a reality men must take into consideration as they decide what to do. Those who turn a blind eye will become the dinosaurs, and, warns one churchwoman, "The dinosaurs die out." After a lifetime of working in the denomination where she can only be a volunteer, one laywoman summarizes this way: "These men, they're going to have to be total men." By this she means, "They're going to have to ask us women what we think—and then listen and follow us. They're going to have to stop being afraid to show emotion, or admit a mistake or love and be tender. The macho thing is over. It's over."

Helping women will cause men to change. It is inevitable, a part of the outcome of diversity. Women will change too, and eventually the patriarchy will change. "In fifty years it will be all different," said one clergywoman hopefully. Women know this; many men know and hope for this too. "I think it's exciting," one churchwoman concludes. "We get the best [of women and men] when all of us can develop our masculine and feminine traits . . . so we're not boxed in to an either/or way of being. There are times to be assertive and times to be nurturing, and God knows, nobody does this right all the time." But when we do get it right, she adds, "The sum is greater than the parts."

— — Chapter Eleven — —

The Mathematics of Power (and Other Equations for Women)

Women are ambivalent about power. They say so over and over again in many different ways.

"I'll use myself as an example," says one churchwoman. "I have a [male] friend who said to me one day, 'Ann,[1] I know that you are more forceful than you allow yourself to be. I think it would be helpful if you were more honest and allowed that forceful part of yourself to come forward.' I thought about that and watched him work and I realized it's true. Men are not afraid of power. They are not afraid to use it."

Another laywoman reports a similar encounter with a male colleague. "A man that I worked with for seventeen years said to me, 'I have never met anyone in all my management years who uses power and authority as judiciously as you do. But you will make a mistake if you don't understand that you have that kind of power.' I thought about that a lot . . . and one of the things I learned from it is to take risks. I will accomplish a lot more."

The ambivalence we women have about power is the wellspring of our problems in the white male system. In order to overcome this, we must take off our blinders and look power directly in the face. It's like slaying the fearful dragon, so difficult is this task for women. It requires that we understand our inner authority as well as the authority given to us as leaders. Then we must learn what power is and isn't, how it works, and how we can use it as women. Once this is done, we can work from a position of strength in doing many other things that will help us succeed as leaders.

Sizing Up the Dragon

The response of women to power is complex. We misinterpret it, fear it, covet it, need it, and at the same time reject it, or at best hold it at a safe distance. "Women are often afraid of power," one laywoman says candidly. "I think in a sense there is a certain amount of dishonesty about this. It's not as though we don't understand it, but we don't use it very directly, and that is not helpful." We may never look it squarely in the face and say, "This is the dragon I must subdue!"

First, we women have been oppressed and abused by power so much and for so long that we unconsciously reject it as a bad thing. When this is pointed out to us, we retort that we don't have any power anyway, and besides, we're not sure we want any. Look what power has done to us and our minority brothers and sisters, we rightly say. "I am concerned that I might hurt someone or leave someone out in the process, and I don't like that," says one churchwoman. The result of this fear, she adds, is that she and other women "have trouble claiming power for ourselves."

THEME THIRTEEN: Women are ambivalent about power.

Women also fear claiming and using power because it might be selfish, destructive, or result in our abandonment.[2] These fears give us away. We are unrelenting caretakers, so that we cannot put aside the needs of others long enough to claim our own power (which is, after all, part of taking care of ourselves).

Second, we know subconsciously that we have a great deal of power that we have been sitting on like a hand grenade in the nest for a long time. Otherwise, we would not believe that our own power will be destructive when (and if) it is finally released. Third, we are complicit in sexism, giving in to being "taken care of" by men. Otherwise we would not fear abandonment (which is different than being alone) so much. These fears are all part of the relationship/care/inadequacy cycle that is such a familiar part of women's lives, and that leads to "surplus powerlessness," a commitment on the part of some women to failure, isolation, and weakness.[3] "We've got to get beyond being victims," in this way, says one clergywoman.

Finally, we often don't claim our own power because it's easier not to take it. We have our own sexism to lean on. We can blame men for our struggle. And we can go on being powerless while we ignore the power that we already have—and that might liberate us. Can we imagine what it would be like if no one questioned our right to ordination? How would we react if gender were no longer a barrier to ordination?[4] Perhaps we do need sexism as much as men do, in our case, to protect us from our fear of or unfamiliarity with taking risks or being in charge. In our frailty we sometimes lack the courage to unhook from men and from the sexism of their system.

If we can get beyond these biases, we are more able to try to generate some power around us. Then the men and their biases trip us up, for it is not just women who contribute to women's avoidance of power. It is men, too, who malign or misinterpret women who want or achieve power. Here's what happens: "First, we get to be embarrassed for even wanting it. Then we get to be attacked in public if we show our interest. Then, after we get it, we get to feel guilty for having it." This happens because, in seeking power, women defy the gender stereotype that is as familiar to us as a mantra: women are trained for private virtue; men for public power.[5] Men, by contrast, always have power—"just enough to trick [them] into thinking it is [their] right."[6]

Women who are at least aware of all these pitfalls of power-seeking find themselves in a situation like the one described by professor Martha Stortz. Paired with an African American pastor to teach an interdisciplinary seminary class, she observes, "What Richard and I found out during the course of the semester was that we were each extremely reluctant to exercise any kind of leadership in the group, particularly in the presence of the other. As a woman and an African American, we had each experienced power largely as domination and oppression. Now that we each had power, we were loath to replicate those past histories for the students in our group, but absolutely clueless about any alternatives."[7]

Three Takes on Power

Setting out to slay the power dragon, women go in the wrong direction right away. At the outset we, "reject a form of power that is accepted and that does work," says one observant laywoman. She is referring to authoritative power, or "power over." This is what we reject, but it is not what has abused us. To get on the right track, we have to back up for some definition.

Power may be "the capacity to produce change." In this definition it means "to be able to do." Those who have power can; they are strong. Those who don't have power can't; they are weak. All of us—women and men—"need power to realize our purpose in ministry." This is often how women define and understand power.[8] But it isn't really this simple. There are at least two other legitimate definitions of power. Failing to differentiate one kind of power from another is how women get off on the wrong track in understanding it. Power can be interpreted, as above, *as capacity*. It can also be understood *as a commodity* or *as relationship*. Power *as capacity* is "power within," or the leader's ability to empower (or dominate) others, as we have seen. Power *as commodity* is "power over," the authoritative power that so often is maligned by women. It is external to the leader, and accumulates or diminishes. In this interpretation, "power is played like a zero-sum game." The more one has, the less there is for others. Women are familiar with this interpretation of power most commonly by observing or participating in the power games of the white male system. Power *as relationship* is "power with." It is based on the interaction of people and organizations to accomplish its ends.

Each of these forms of power is legitimate and useful. The abuse of any one of them is illegitimate and not useful for effective leadership.[9] This is the point we miss in understanding power. A generic definition might be "power is realized capacity."[10] There are many ways to realize capacity, as we have seen here, depending on situations, relationships, individuals, and structures. Any one of the ways of realizing capacity can be abused.

We fall into confusion most often in our understanding of authoritative power. "Power over" is the dominant definition of power understood in leadership circles, inside and outside the denominations. "We still believe the conventional wisdom that 'power over' is how ministry should be done."[11] It is also that which we most often experience as abusive. We fall into error when we assume that *the abuse of* "power over" is the main event. It isn't. There are legitimate applications of authoritative power, the most obvious being the parent-child relationship. "Power over" is not evil, inappropriate, or destructive unless it is abused. Because we are unaware of this, we often refuse to see the legitimacy of "power over" in any application,[12] or at worst, consider all power, no matter what kind it is, as abusive.[13] Contributing to this tendency is some discomfort with power as capacity to get things done—"power within." It can be abusive as well when it is used to dominate rather than empower others. We may therefore reject it in the same way that we reject "power over."

When we women cut ourselves off from authoritative power, we put ourselves in a position of weakness. When we reject power as capacity ("power within") as well, we have only one option left: power as relationship, or "power with," the most diffuse and undefined of the forms of power, and the one least understood in leadership circles. We are left to deal with its limitations, its tendency to be exclusionary of outsiders and its political amorphism. Thus, in our effort to avoid any use of power that has historically abused us, we may indeed fall into a trap: "A kind of personal, structureless politics; widespread opposition to leadership *of any kind;* an insistence on working collectively; and an emphasis on process, often to the exclusion of getting things done."[14]

The only way out of this trap is to take a wider view of power and its possibilities. The bottom line, says one laywoman: "We women are fooling ourselves. We really do have power, and we do exercise that power over other people, including other women. We have to come to terms with the kinds of power we do have and the fact that we can abuse power as much as men. [Then] we have to decide how we are going to use the power we have."

Claiming Our Authority

Authority is given to us to help us claim our legitimate power. It can come from many sources. Ordination is one. Election and installation to public office is another. Authority may also be granted informally, as it is to parents who are recognized by the social community and the law as having authority over (and responsibility for) their children. There are many examples of authority externally conferred. Thinking about these shows how obviously authority places our power in the context of community.[15]

Women do benefit by the conferring of external authority. As an example, we often have an easier time exercising our pastoral power from the pulpit because ordination gives us the authority to do so.[16] But I would contend that this is not enough. Women must also have an inner authority that comes from legitimizing ourselves. Otherwise, we are always like the pastor who writes that she, like many women, "thinks that something will come in the mail saying there has been a mistake and that, in fact, I am not ordained."[17] No amount of authority granted by whatever powers-that-be will help us claim our power unless we first go public with that which makes us unique as women in leadership.[18] Then we will be empowered by the external authority conferred upon us.

This requires audacity. The unique power of women in leadership comes from many things, most of which are absent from the list of "most desired traits" in the patriarchy. We have to give our uniqueness value by using it proudly and displaying it for all (including, yes, men) to see. That's how we legitimize our own authority. The criteria for our authority includes our ability to focus on the whole, our comfort with relationships, a process orientation, a willingness to share information and thereby empower others, the intimacy we bring to the workplace, and our risk taking. These criteria are, of course, the very things that women described as aspects of their leadership styles in chapter 2.

In order to make our uniqueness more valuable, we have to stop keeping it a secret. We must instead "go public." This starts with how we talk and ends up being a way we think and know ourselves. "For us to obtain authority as women . . . we must risk making generalizations."[19] Our comfort is in applying what we know about leadership only to ourselves or the particular situation. ("*My* style is to do *my* homework, listen to others, but at the same time, stick to *my* principles.") Women have spoken this way in this very book. We become uncomfortable when we try to generalize. ("Leaders should do *their* homework. Part of that is listening to others instead of making decisions in isolation.") We don't want to force this point of view on anyone else. Perhaps we don't even feel sure enough about our leadership to risk generalizing about it at all. Our tendency to particularize in this way weakens us. It limits the authority of our own style to us or to a particular situation.

We are keeping our own criteria for leadership a secret when we particularize. Instead we must hold up our criteria and say not only that they are good for us, but that they are good for all leaders. Men generalize like this all the time. We women are often offended when they do. But we cannot claim that men are doing wrong in generalizing what they know about leadership. Nor can we deny that men have gained by doing so. They claim community and establish a common knowledge about what makes a leader when they generalize. We, on the other hand, choose isolation, the private understanding of leadership that never means anything to anyone but us. Thus, we deny ourselves authority. We don't claim it for ourselves, and we don't get it from external sources.

Learning from Men

If women have the courage to go public, we can then learn two skills from men that "can help women come to grips with what it means to have a powerful job and use that power effectively," says one laywoman. Men can teach us to be direct and to be unapologetically ambitious.

"We need to be clear about what we want and what we need and who we are," says another churchwoman. That's being direct. We can practice clarity most simply by speaking our mind in statements, not questions, and then shutting up. Allow the uncomfortable silences that come when we are direct. Allow ourselves to be uncomfortable in those silences until we get the hang of being direct. "This business of trying to second guess other people's feelings has not been productive for us as leaders," one woman says candidly. She advocates being direct and accepting differences that are a normal part of the work environment.

The benefit of such directness, a clergywoman points out is: "If your attitude says, when you really get down to it, 'Don't mess with me,' I think people know that." A clergyman adds that men cannot help women unless they are direct. "We sense that women want more, but if they don't say so, we're caught. We don't want to take advantage of them," he insists. But he and his male colleagues get caught in a dominant position without enough direct input from women.

Another clergywoman in an administrative position reflected on what she has learned about the value of directness. "While my natural style is to get people to do things collaboratively, I've gotten more astute about it, particularly so that I do not get into a crusade and then crash and burn and blame the men or the church for not allowing [collaboration] to work. A dose of realism has helped me." She admits that cynicism is a temptation of this path, "I have also learned every step of the way how little trust is lying around to be picked up. But I've just got to handle my own feelings sometimes and keep putting one foot in front of the other and outlaugh them all the way." The value of humor for women, which she hints at here, we shall come to later.

Ambition is another skill that women often address with ambivalence. We can also learn about it from men. "Work hard until you get it done." That's the formula one clergywoman offers. The attitude behind her energy: "I know that I can do things, and I can probably do [many things] better than anybody in the room, and if nobody else is going to volunteer, I'm going to do it, and I'm going to do it really well." She learned this from her father, she adds.

Men affirm this view for women. For one thing, they know that women still have to be better than men to succeed. "It's not fair; it's not right; it's not just; but it's still a fact," said one layman, "so hone your professional skills to the point that you can be recognized," he advises women. Another concurs. "Refuse to acknowledge the glass ceiling. Dare to be the best and work to be that," he says, adding that women should do this *as women*, not necessarily as men would. "It takes a rare combination of being tough but oh-so-gentle, to be out in front and still collegial."

Other Equations for Women

It's as though we have to learn to engage our masculine side and then return to what our feminine birthright has to teach us. Once authoritative as a result of "going public," being more direct and becoming unapologetically ambitious, we can become powerful in many ways that do not deny who we are as women.

Take pride in the power we have. Women's groups raise millions of dollars for the denominations, provide a wide range of services, and engage in very creative ministries. This is power. In most denominations, however, these women's organizations are still second class, their leaders considered less powerful than mainstream (male) leaders. In some denominations, the women's groups themselves get co-opted back into the mainstream, where men hold the power. This neutralizes the work and influence of women entirely.

Women could also elect most or all of the leaders in some denominations if they wanted to, so predominant are women in the work and life of the church. This is power too. But "we have to get together and be a little more strategic," says one laywoman in frustration. "Too many women have grown up thinking this is wrong; we shouldn't strategize that way, and so we can't do it. We don't even empower ourselves."

As these examples point out, we are quick to say that it is "not our style" to take over, and we are double quick to ensure that the work we do serves the whole church, not just ourselves. I have no argument with this stance. We are far ahead of men in having it. But we hurt ourselves too. We are so quick to put ourselves in the servant role that we do not always recognize and use the power we already have. Too often then, we get duped into giving it away. The result: what we women could do with our own power to change the position of women in the church never gets done. We leave the men in charge when we allow their power and deny our own.

Speak up. "Speech against structures creates change. Silence does not."[20] Women need to speak up. We are so used to being quiet or, what's little better, allowing ourselves to be silenced after we have already spoken. We get tired. Says one churchwoman of many years, "All women, no matter where we are in leadership, have a repeat experience of not being taken seriously. You go into a new setting with people who don't know you, and no matter how much experience you have, you feel that sometimes you have to start all over again. . . . I feel like I have to sell myself rather than just being accepted for who I am. It never stops for me." Women in leadership know what she means. Still, we have to speak up.

Surely, a part of speaking up effectively is speaking in a language that men can understand. So all women learn to speak white male. We also know how to speak female. Some of us know how to talk white and talk black. But we must also remember that "truly authoritative women would insist on talking their own language all the time, even among men."[21] This challenge reminds me of a woman in very senior circles in one denomination who often used the metaphor of cleaning house to explain to the men what needed to be done. They didn't like it, but they learned from it all the same. And they also learned a little bit about speaking *her* language.

Notice differences among women. This requires listening. It seems we do so much listening. We listen to men. We listen to systems that debate around us about our suitability for ministry. I would urge that we focus our listening on each other. We need to get to know how women are different from each other. It's important because "there is a key generational difference among women clergy now, with the younger trusting way too much in the women's movement to guarantee security and the older generation much too burned by the trouble we've already seen. There are so many interesting ways to be mistaken."[22] I would contend that this is true not only for clergy but for all churchwomen. Another thing that's different now for younger women is summarized by an older churchwoman: "They don't necessarily have to be the first. They don't have to break the barrier, but on the other hand . . . the more people get used to women, the more I think some of the problems [women have] get ignored." She adds that younger women have unique struggles balancing private and professional lives, while older women often did their mothering and then became professionals.

There's so much more here—differences for women of minority races who face triple jeopardy in negotiating the white male system, differences among lay and clergy women, differences among women in conservative denominations, and more. "Blacks and whites, rich and poor, male and female, we are not a people and we have no mutual God."[23] It is essential that we begin to know and trust each other as women.

Mentor other women. When we know each other, we can mentor each other. We women, just like men, need mentors to succeed in becoming leaders and to help us define what leadership is for us.[24] Surely we can learn from men, but to define ourselves and our style as different from men's (rather than deviant from men's) we need the mentoring of other women. There is great benefit for us in mentoring. We can tell each other our stories. We can speak our own language freely. "I think women learn differently than men. I would want to give them the assurance that they don't have to be anything else but themselves," says one laywoman.

This is precisely why one lifelong volunteer in church leadership has been committed to helping other women become leaders too. "My

THEME FOURTEEN: Women need mentoring.

leadership was not just to get things done, but to develop others to be able to continue that leadership," she says. "We are always trying to reach out to all women."

A younger woman just entering church leadership explains why she sought female mentors: "I wanted to see how women do it differently, particularly how women could have power and make it work." From her mentors she has learned, "that it is possible for women to be in leadership positions." It's elementary but essential to know this.

"For whatever reason, women have not always been secure enough to mentor other women," says another, who has been a mentor herself. "We would be far better off if we would say, 'Yes, I am strong enough and I am committed enough, and I am productive enough. I can mentor other women and it will not damage me one bit.' "

Be ourselves boldly. One woman asks, "How can we be in positions of leadership and still be dangerous leaders?" The answer, it seems to me, is that we must be true to our own way as leaders.[25] Another churchwoman puts it succinctly. "The secret of being a successful woman is to be a woman." Here I raise a caution about the things we learn from men. What we learn from them we must use as women. The balance is subtle.

We must learn to survive in the patriarchy, to be sure. We can survive by not becoming overinvolved in the housekeeping tasks of the denominations. Next, a delicate counterpoint to learning from men to be direct and ambitious is that we must not try to do everything so thoroughly and so well. Third, we should share the relational tasks that need to be done with the men. Fourth, we must expect more from men and less from women. Above all, we must learn to focus on significant achievements. These skills require women to "resist their internal radar," and "reinforce behaviors that are more directly task related."[26]

At the same time, we must continue to be ourselves and thereby to challenge the patriarchy. This is what is required of dangerous leaders. We do so by "going public" with our own style, holding it up as a useful model for men as well as women. We do so by allowing women a growing diversity of leadership styles. We do so over and over again when we speak our own leadership language. We do so when we make a commitment to be audacious. One young woman concludes, "It's really important to be yourself, to be comfortable with yourself, not to try to fit a certain role."

Allow distance for our female leaders. "Women in leadership positions need to learn how to befriend one another. Women who are following women or who are relating to women in leadership positions need to learn to keep a distance," says one laywoman now in leadership herself. Too often we expect women leaders to be familiar friends, close to the rest of us who are the followers. We thus deny them the distance that authority requires. The result is that we hurt their chances to be effective leaders for men as well as women.

Furthermore, women in leadership need to become comfortable with all kinds of power, including "power over" others. This particularly requires distance. "Awareness of this kind of power separates the leader from the group and the ordained minister from the congregation. It forces the leader to deal with differences; differences that are really inherent in the office. To pretend away such differences would be an act of denial." This in fact is one of the limitations of power as relationship ("power with"). It denies "differences in power between leader and group. It also denies responsibilities that rest—and rest only—with the leader."[27]

Keep on keeping on. Women have to be there, in the leadership of the church. This is demanding. We women working in the patriarchy suffer the stress of working in a male dominated system, a stress that causes depression, weariness, and discouragement, and that ranges from "mildly irritating" to crippling of our leadership.[28] It is also demanding of our time and energy. But when we are there, things begin to change. Eventually, thanks to the presence of women and minorities in leadership, the patriarchy will give way to new systems.

One clergywoman talked of the influence of her presence in her congregation. "I'm here. I'm up at the altar every Sunday and the little kids draw pictures and [in them] there's a girl behind the altar. I think those are the girls that grow up without ever having a clue that being a pastor means being a man. They won't even understand that there was a time women couldn't do this."

Laugh as Sarah laughed. When Sarah overheard God talking to Abraham about her impending pregnancy, she laughed. I do not believe she was being impudent, nor was she mocking God. She was laughing, as women must laugh, at the irony of her life. She was laughing at finally gaining what she had long ago given up. She was laughing that God told Abraham and not her. She was laughing because otherwise she would have to cry.

It helps for women to have a sense of humor about the ridiculousness of bureaucracies that quibble over "what we can do." Bureaucracies don't have a sense of humor. Men sometimes don't either. They are often too threatened by women to share their humor in mixed gender settings, or, more sadly, they don't know any humor that isn't sexist or outright sexually suggestive. Healthy, robust humor about our predicament in the patriarchy falls to the women. We should laugh and remember Sarah.

Be angry and be merciful. We are most powerful as women when we "require the church and society to repent of their sins against us as women, while standing ready to forgive and receive the transformation that implies."[29] Think for a moment of the men or systems that have most abused us. Then imagine how we might forgive them at the same time that we refuse to let them abuse us again. If we can do this, we have found a measure of mercy in our own rage. This is absolutely required. Without it, we remain partners with those men and systems in our continuing abuse. With it, we are ready for a new way of leadership that we can share with men without abuse.

Finding a New Way

If we can remember some of these things all of the time, and maybe all of them some of the time, we are ready for a new way. "In the Protestant church, I see our job as creating a new field and not merely sending women down to play with the boys." Surely this is what we hope for. "Most of us really [don't] want to play on the same old field, but on a transformed one."[30] Says one churchwoman, "I really think that the one thing that could be done to improve the situation for women anywhere, is for women and men to work together as peers."

Another young woman adds her own goal for the future. "The most important thing is to figure out some level of authenticity that enables me to work in relationships with all types of people."

Chapter Twelve

Our Own Wisdom

Bob, Elizabeth, Jeff, and the staff who worked with them at Advent Church did a lot of things right when they began working together. They also did many things wrong. By now we know what most of those things are, and we know why things went so wrong for no obvious reason. The question remains, however: What must happen in order for women and men to have a more effective and mutually satisfying ministry with each other?

I asked men and women to discuss this question together and to share their answers in a systematic way. Their responses can help us rewrite the story of Advent.

Ten Factors for Change

There are ten factors for change that emerged from the discussions of church leaders throughout the established denominations. They verify many of the specific suggestions in chapters 10 and 11, so much so that they provide a good summary for us.

FACTOR ONE: **Reflection comes first, then action.** Action will accomplish little, churchwomen and men say, until reflection has borne fruit. All the things that Bob and Elizabeth and Jeff did to begin their ministry together were necessary, but should not have been first. Church leadership calls for a number of reflective activities: repenting of the past, speaking the truth to each other, listening, getting to know one another better, becoming aware of gender and individual differences, and actively seeking God's will for women and men. All of these reflective activities should help us become more aware of each other in a deeper way.

The deeper awareness that comes from reflective activity goes beyond knowing each other by what we do to knowing each other for who we are and what we are like. This kind of knowing requires acceptance of gender differences and individual differences within genders. It also requires a willingness to know ourselves better. It is only achieved by a great deal of listening. It takes time. Our prayerful repentance is a prerequisite for this deeper knowing of one another.

FACTOR TWO: Women and men must acknowledge each other. As an outgrowth of the reflective tasks, church leaders recognize the need for mutual acknowledgment. It may seem obvious that men and women need to do this, but it isn't apparent as part of the daily grind. Sad as it is, women and men have been working with each other for a long time without knowing or truly acknowledging each other. At Advent Church, Bob and Jeff and Elizabeth began their work without understanding what it might mean to have a mixed gender staff. The tasks of acknowledgment include respect, a recognition that both men and women have a legitimate calling to ministry (of clergy or laity), and assignment of value to the other. It is the opposite of the "ungifting" that we so often do to each other. True acknowledgment would free both women and men from stereotypes.

FACTOR THREE: Sexism, racism, and other prejudices must be named and addressed. This painful step cannot be overlooked. Even if we reflect together and acknowledge each other, not much positive benefit can be gained unless women and men both repent of the sins of sexism and racism. This requires the personal admission from each of us that we are sexist and we are racist, and is particularly necessary if we are members of the dominant group. It is sexism and racism that tempt us to use discrimination to cover other deeper issues, including our own fear of each other. When Elizabeth came to Advent Church, Alice's rejection of her was based on her acceptance of secondary status for herself and for all women. This was sexism that Alice did not recognize. Each of the other staff members had sexist attitudes that got in the way as well.

Many white persons have said that they became free to work against racism only when they admitted, at least to themselves and God, their own racist attitudes. Many men also say that they lose their defensiveness toward women when they admit in the same private way their unavoidable sexist attitudes. When we have admitted these "isms," we can embrace diversity with the knowledge that everyone is changed by it. The minority persons change as they come into the sphere of the majority, and the majority persons are changed, too, by the positive influence of the minority. True diversity is accomplished only when all persons are changed. This never happened at Advent. When it does happen, we can begin to lead the church together in a "new way" without defensiveness.

FACTOR FOUR: Women and men must be together in the same work setting. This is coexistence. It may seem simple. Reflecting together, acknowledging each other, finding a new way, all the tasks of change require being together in the same space, working together, day after day. If this were so simple, we would not have denominations that deny women access to leadership. If this were so simple, we would be able to achieve it without "quotas" to force us. Since it isn't simple, we need to be intentional, as the leadership at Advent was. Intentionality requires actively recruiting women in particular, since they are still underrepresented in church leadership. How we do this may or may not involve quotas, depending mostly on our level of commitment to it.

Working together successfully also includes mentoring each other. Mentoring relationships would have helped the team avoid and overcome their hurdles, and possibly succeed. Men need to learn from women about working with women. Women need to learn from men about working with men. Women also need to learn from other women about claiming their own style at the same time that they work in a male-defined workplace.

FACTOR FIVE: We all need more education. Both men and women need to know more about gender differences; about the actual situation of women in the church today; about Jesus' relationships to women friends and disciples; about the women leaders of the early church who have been left out of the Bible; about what women in church leadership today have to offer, and how men struggle to understand it. There is so much to learn together. None of this learning happened at Advent Church, except by accident.

In addition, as long as women work in a male-defined workplace, they need leadership development skills training to help them in two ways. First, many women need the opportunity to develop leadership skills that have been overlooked or suppressed by limited early education and lack of opportunity later in life. Second, they need to learn how to work successfully in a "foreign" environment. Women have much to learn from men. While women are learning these things, men could be learning more about how women lead and how to adapt their dominant styles to integrate women better. Men can learn from women too. Ultimately, both men and women need to learn new styles of leading together, styles that combine the best of what both have to offer.

FACTOR SIX: Power must be understood and used differently. Instead of something to hoard lest we run out, power must be shared so that all might have more. We all need to view power as abundant. This is largely a task for men, requiring a change in their view of power. The whole story of Advent might have been different if Bob had viewed the power of the senior pastor role differently. In a different paradigm, he might not have reserved the decisions about preaching assignments for himself in the first place.

For women, the task is somewhat different but just as difficult. We must stop fearing power and learn to welcome our own unique power as an ally. Elizabeth might have spoken up sooner and more forcefully—and also less emotionally—if she had been comfortable with her own power and its effect on the others in her team.

Before either gender can accomplish these tasks, we must both understand how power is used now, and particularly how the abuse of power hurts women. Power "games" must stop.

FACTOR SEVEN: Theological issues must be addressed. Theology is so often used against women that saying so is like asserting that the sky is blue. But in many real situations, it's hard to see how theology affects underlying attitudes. Why, for instance, should anyone in the Advent congregation have had reservations about "seeing a woman in the pulpit"? Our denominations' centuries-old teachings about the proper roles of women have a profound effect on our attitudes, whether we are aware of it or not. As we have seen, theology is central to these teachings.

In many denominations, it is not just underlying attitudes. Theological stance overtly bars women from leadership or severely limits their role. In order for theological abuse to stop, we must learn to distinguish between theology, culture, and tradition. We must not mistake sociology for theology. We must remain true to the whole of scripture, and we must not wear out our theology to prove a point. In some settings, these changes will require an entirely new theological paradigm. In all settings, they call us to return to the scriptures.

FACTOR EIGHT: Inclusive language will help. Language is the embodiment of our thoughts, our ideas, our way of conceptualizing the world. Elizabeth knew that when she tried to make small changes in the language of hymns, and some of her choir members objected. Language reflects attitude, and we must be sensitive about language if we are serious about the equality of women. If women were included in leadership equally, our language would reflect this by becoming more inclusive. To help us along the way, some attention to the inclusivity of our language will be useful, even when it seems artificial.

Language can also help us name a variety of experiences of the Divine. If we can name God as other than Man or Father, we will be able to expand our understanding of what is ultimately unknowable. There are a thousand names for God and we don't know them all. We must remember as we image God in language that God said, "I am who I am."

FACTOR NINE: New models are required. It's not a matter of women learning hierarchical leadership or men learning to be more relational. Bob couldn't change who he was as a leader in order to make the workplace more comfortable for Elizabeth. Nor should Elizabeth train herself to think, act and work more like Bob or Jeff. It's ultimately a matter of finding new leadership styles that both men and women can appreciate, understand, and use. Once we do this, gender inclusive leadership will be easier.

Openness and flexibility to change, to taking a chance on new ways of leadership, are required for our future as denominations. We can't afford to waste the talent of a single person, male or female. As we look at leadership with a "new way" in mind, we become more and more gender blind, focusing on the gifts we have at our disposal rather than male, female, black, white, or anything else. Our goal is making a team, becoming a working community, not "my way" or "your way."

FACTOR TEN: Individual change is not enough. Systems must change. Lest we all assume that if we just work hard enough things will change, the point must be made. At a time when the church culture is changing cataclysmically, it is not enough for individuals to do their best. The denominations as systems must change as well. Even if everything had gone right at Advent, there are many other mixed gender ministry teams and many other women and men working in lay positions together who are not succeeding.

We need models for authority that are not hierarchical. We need salaries for women that equal those of men for comparable work. We need policies and practices that will bring women into leadership and free them to do their best work. We need to experience partnership and collegiality in our workplace. These tasks are structural. They cannot be achieved by individuals working alone. They start with individuals, but require many people working together on the structure of our churches to be accomplished.

Where Is the Promised Land?

When we enumerate these change factors, the list includes nothing more than the things we said we were going to do a decade or even a generation ago. It is a list we should have mastered by now. Can it be that after all these eleven chapters, there is no surprising and satisfying resolution to the problems that have been so thoroughly examined? Paradoxically, this is exactly the point. Like Moses who was not allowed to enter the Promised Land, we are rendered impotent by our inability to change. We are still in the wilderness.

The tasks remain before us. This is the unmistakable message from women and men in leadership. There are three good reasons. First, the change factors have no real meaning for us yet. They are still words in a list, not lessons branded into our hearts. Who among us has reflected for forty days in a personal wilderness about what it might mean to listen? Who has ever truly experienced what it means to acknowledge another person, a coworker of the opposite sex? Who has unpeeled the layers of his—or her—own sexism? Until we do these things from the heart, the tasks of reflection, acknowledgment, and naming the "isms" remain undone.

Second, we cannot take any action successfully until reflection has changed us from within. This we know from the list itself. We are all in danger of rushing for the quick fix. Like the men described earlier, we either "don't get it" or we want to fix it now. Like Jesus in the wilderness, we are tempted to do something, to make the Kingdom come. It is much harder to wait, listen, and reflect.

Third, and most problematic, our systems lack the vitality for change. Even if we as individuals could do something, our systems would fail us in the end. Burdened by their own institutionalized sins, which trap both women and men, our church hierarchies are too overweight and overwrought to adapt. Like the temple that Jesus cleansed in a rage, they must be swept clean in favor of something new. We are living in a time of "sweeping clean."

What we will come to after the sweeping away is not yet clear to us, and that's the final problem. When we cannot imagine the future, it is hard to describe what we need to do to get there. Language is a poor communicator for what is not yet apparent. What we need right now are not solutions, but silence, and the space to imagine what we might be like if we were different—if someone in some church somewhere could do the things that the change factors enumerate. What is left to us is a question: What would Advent Church be like if . . .

Rewriting the Story of Advent Church

Pastor Bob had been at Advent for six years when he began to think about bringing a woman into the ministry there. He felt that the leadership of the congregation was open to the possibility. Where there was resistance, he believed that with help, he could overcome it. He began to pray about this. He thought about himself, the strong and capable women who had influenced his life, and his own attitudes about women. He decided to try to get to know a woman pastor in his clergy cluster better and eventually asked her to help him become more aware of issues and concerns of women in ministry, as well as to tell him when he was being sexist himself. Then he began reading—feminist theologies, women in the Bible, sermons by women. When an occasion arose, he went to a seminar taught by women and about women in ministry. Finally, he began keeping a journal.

Pastor Bob shared his idea with Jeff, the education minister who was much younger than he. Jeff had ideas of his own, and some insights that were helpful. Sometimes, though, Bob noticed that Jeff resisted the idea. He seemed threatened. Bob invited Jeff to join him in study and reflection. Eventually they included Alice and Sandy in their reflections. Alice was huffy about it at first, but she did participate. Together, the staff planned a Bible study series on women in ministry for the congregation. It included a look at theological issues related to women in ministry. It lasted six weeks and was open to those who wanted to come. The group was small the first time around, but by the third time the series was offered, several months had gone by and others in the congregation had heard how good it was. The group was large, including both women and men.

It was a year later when the congregation decided that they were ready to add a third pastor to the staff. They would hire a specialist in music. Bob had learned enough by this time to know that he should not announce or even suggest that "this pastor will be a woman." He did work actively to keep the idea alive, and he knew that his work and the work of the staff had prepared the congregation well. When they found Elizabeth and decided to call her to the position, Bob was excited and pleased, but apprehensive too. He had taken the first step, but this was just the beginning.

When Elizabeth became the new associate and the first woman pastor at Advent Church, her arrival meant something personal to everyone on the staff and to many in the congregation. They worked hard to welcome her. They also knew that her arrival would mean change for them. It was a "new day" at Advent.

During the first week, Elizabeth learned many important things about the parish, the volunteer committees, the office procedures, the preaching schedule for the next few months, and the issues facing the congregation in the immediate future. In turn, the staff had a chance to get to know more about Elizabeth and what she would be doing in her specialty as music director/pastor.

Elizabeth settled in. She was happy to be part of a team. In her first call, she had been alone in a very small parish. It had been lonely for a single woman. Then she had returned to graduate school to study church music. This made her a more attractive candidate for a team ministry and allowed her to enjoy her love of music. At Advent, she got off to a great start with the choirs and did many things to enhance the music programs of the congregation. Her efforts to change the language of the hymns so they would be more inclusive met with some resistance but no open controversy. There were discussions and mutual decisions about what to change and what to leave alone. Elizabeth had her committee assignments, her visits to the sick and shut-ins and all the routine tasks of an associate to keep her very busy.

In addition to these routine tasks of getting to know the congregation, Elizabeth and Bob and Jeff set aside some specific times that they would work together to become a team. At least once a month this included other members of the staff, who were part of the team as well. This time was spent over the next months getting to know each other as partners and people. They talked about their leadership styles, their coming to the ministry, and their hopes for the congregation. They even had two sessions with a local psychologist to evaluate what each could contribute to the team ministry. Gradually, Bob and Elizabeth formed a mentoring relationship that helped them both learn. Elizabeth also had a nearby clergywoman to mentor her, the woman whom Bob had gotten to know in his clergy cluster so many months ago when he started this project.

In the days and months after Elizabeth joined the staff at Advent, she learned a great deal more about the daily life of the congregation, the groups who used the building on weekdays, the life and work of the parish committees, the youth, the choirs, the worship schedule and liturgies, and of course the individual people and their concerns—so many things that are part of the routine of pastoring and caring for a congregation. She also learned a great deal about working with male colleagues. Bob and Jeff, in turn, were learning about working with a female associate and what that would mean for them and the congregation. Alice changed too. She began to think of doing some things she had never done since her husband died, things she never thought she could do alone. Harold was surprised at what a pleasure it was to work with Elizabeth. He enjoyed noticing the ways she was different from young Pastor Jeff. Sandy made plans to go back to college part-time.

Bob did not give up his style of senior pastoring, nor did he feel that it was necessary. Sure, he discussed things with Jeff and Elizabeth and often with the women working in the office as well. At least once a month the whole staff had a meeting together. But Bob made some decisions himself, after discussion with the others. One of those decisions was preaching assignments. He typically gave Jeff and Elizabeth each three preaching assignments in a quarter and took six himself. He was aware after six months that he did have some concerns about Elizabeth's preaching. Partly he knew it was just different than his. Partly, he still had to admit it was strange to see a woman in the pulpit. When he began hearing similar reactions from some of the people in the congregation, he was tempted to deal with it simply by cutting back a little bit on Elizabeth's preaching assignments. That was the easiest thing to do, and it didn't seem like a very big deal to him.

Instead, Bob did just the opposite. He decided to increase Elizabeth's role in presiding at worship so that she would become more familiar as a figure of authority in the pastoral leadership of the congregation. He knew that providing her more of a presence in worship was the best way to do this. At the same time, he and the other two pastors all planned a second series on women in leadership, this time focusing on the women who had been instrumental in the early church. All these steps seemed to help.

Building a team in this way starts with everyone looking inside instead of outside. But this isn't just "touchy feely stuff." It is hard work and the stakes are high. Bob and his colleagues found out that everyone became personally accountable when they started with themselves. Bob himself became a congruent leader. It was therefore possible for true teaming to happen even though individual members of the team retained their human frailties and limitations. At the same time, the success of the team did not mean life was perfect. As the staff at Advent found out, being successful with a new paradigm raises suspicion in others. This team actually found that its relationship with the denomination became more difficult for awhile. They were, after all, breaking the old molds. But they each knew that they were also engaging in personal behavior that opened up a whole new way of leadership together.

There was much ahead for Bob and his team. Except for the small changes the choir had made in some hymns, they had not yet tackled the difficult and sometimes divisive issue of more inclusive language in worship. He knew that was necessary. They saw in their area many other congregations that were not succeeding as well with mixed gender teams, and they were dismayed. They also saw some denominational policies that definitely needed to be changed in order for mixed gender teams to have a better chance of getting started and succeeding. Their questions about those policies were not always welcome. Sometimes, in fact, they felt like outsiders in their own denomination because they were building a team in such a different way and succeeding. There were still challenges ahead for this relatively new team. But it was, nevertheless, a team that was succeeding in ministry together.

Epilogue

This epilogue could be a list of the one hundred most obvious things I did wrong when I worked (with men) in my denomination. I am appalled at all the ways I was misunderstood. They have come to me gradually, like a mental list, as I have interviewed other women and men in leadership. A list of the things I did right (from men's point of view) would be much shorter. Probably no more than ten points.

It is instructive to have this hindsight. What I do with it now is most important. If I wallow in "what I did wrong," or even come to believe that I did things all wrong because men misinterpreted me, I am on the wrong track. In fact, I did a lot of things—most things—exactly right. It's just that the men didn't know it. And where I did go wrong is that I failed to help them understand me.

As a minority person in the white male culture, it *was* my responsibility to help the majority interpret my leadership correctly. I didn't. I didn't know it was necessary. I didn't know how. In some cases, I was unwilling to take on the task.

Having gained this insight the hard way, I believe that there are three alternatives for us as women. One is to lead as we will and throw interpretation to the wind. Perhaps in some cases it doesn't matter if the men understand what we are about. The second is to deny our own ways of leading and adopt not only the style but the moral stance of men. For me, both of these are unacceptable. I would choose the third way, a way I have come to understand by hearing the stories of many other women.

We choose to be women, to lead as women, and proudly to interpret our style to men as they need that interpretation. We can also dream of a day when we won't have the task of explaining ourselves all the time.

— — Notes — —

Introduction

1. Donna Schaper, *Common Sense About Men and Women in the Ministry* (Washington, D.C.: The Alban Institute, 1990), 10.
2. I consider women volunteers leaders in the church just as much as those who are paid to serve, though many have reported to me that they do not consider themselves leaders. Apparently their denominations' policies have caused them to think of themselves as just volunteers and not leaders at all.
3. Mary Kay Belenky, et al., *Women's Ways of Knowing* (New York: Basic Books, 1986), 131-38.
4. Carol E. Becker, "Women in Church Leadership: An Emerging Paradigm," *Leading the Congregation* by Norman Shawchuck and Roger Heuser (Nashville: Abingdon Press, 1993), 253-77. I was employed by the Evangelical Lutheran Church in America at the time this article was drafted.
5. *The Lutheran*, January 1995, 49.
6. Schaper, *Common Sense About Men and Women in the Ministry*, 69.

Part One—Leadership Embodied

1. Lutheran judicatories did not offer ordination to women until 1970. In 1972, the time of this story, the first few women were being educated for the Lutheran ministry. It took many more years for women with other careers to return to seminary and later become ordained.
2. Martha Ellen Stortz identifies power over, power within, and power with, all as legitimate forms of power. She identifies the authority that comes with each. See *Pastor Power* (Nashville: Abingdon Press, 1993).
3. Jeannette Sherrill, "Power and Authority: Issues for Women Clergy as Leaders" (Middlesex, N.Y.: Hartford Seminary doctoral dissertation, 1990), 93.
4. Letty Russell, *Church in the Round* (Louisville: Westminster/John Knox Press, 1993), 55. See also Stortz, 51.
5. See also R. Roosevelt Thomas, *Beyond Race and Gender* (New York: American Management Association, 1991) and Cornel West, *Race Matters* (Boston: Beacon Press, 1993). Both of these African American writers speak eloquently about this phenomenon in relation to racial prejudice. It is our concern in this book to address the gender issues.
6. Russell, *Church in the Round*, 55.

7. For a thought-provoking essay on the tasks of Christian leadership, see Jackson Carroll, *As One With Authority* (Louisville: Westminster/John Knox Press, 1991), chapter 5, "The Central Tasks of Leadership in the Church."

1. What Church Women and Men Say About Leadership

1. This story, which provides an example of the kinds of problems women face in church leadership, is fictitious, based on many anecdotes and incidents shared by women. Of all the situations in this book, this is the only one that is not based on actual fact.

2. Women Leading in the Church

1. In a study of male-female mixed gender teams, Betty Jane Bailey found that most characteristics "have less to do with gender than with senior/associate relationships in general." See "The Mixed Gender Multiple Staff: Problem or Partnership?" (Chicago: McCormick Seminary Doctoral Dissertation, 1987), 32. I would contend that relationship characteristics are gender related because women are more concerned about maintaining relationships.
2. Letty Russell, *Church in the Round* (Louisville: Westminster/John Knox Press, 1993), 67.
3. Matthew Fox, in a letter to the author.
4. Donna Schaper, *Common Sense About Men and Women in the Ministry* (Washington, D.C.: The Alban Institute, 1990), 5.
5. Edward C. Lehman, Jr., *Gender and Work: The Case of the Clergy* (New York: State University of New York Press, 1993), 20.
6. See chapter 3 for a discussion of cultural paradigms and how these have an impact on women's leadership.
7. Bailey asserts that with their increasing numbers, women in ordained ministry "seem to have more freedom than men to redefine the ministerial role," even though they meet resistance. "The Mixed Gender Multiple Staff: Problem or Partnership?" 5-6. I would note that women in both the church and secular leadership roles get plenty of advice about "how to succeed." Most of this advice focuses on teaching women how to copy men's style because, after all, we still work in a male defined environment.
8. Bailey asserts that this kind of partnership in collaborative leadership is really a mandate for the parish team. "The Mixed Gender Multiple Staff: Problem or Partnership?" 24-5.
9. We will discuss how this affects both men and women in part 2.
10. Bailey's study notes the desire of mixed gender staff to allow a divergence of style. This, she surmises, "may reflect an honoring of gender differences as real." See Bailey, "The Mixed Gender Multiple Staff: Problem or Partnership?" 35.

3. Leadership Paradigms and Women as Leaders

1. Norman Shawchuck and Roger Heuser, *Leading the Congregation* (Nashville: Abingdon Press, 1993), 222.
2. C. S. Lewis, "Imagination and Thought in the Middle Ages," *Chaucer and His Contemporaries*, ed. Helaine Newstead (Greenwich, Conn.: Fawcett, 1968), 47.
3. Raymond Phineas Stearns, *Pageant of Europe: Sources and Selections from the Renaissance to the Present Day* (New York: Harcourt, Brace & World, 1961), 63 and Williston Walker, *A History of the Christian Church* (New York: Scribner's, 1970), 426.
4. Elizabeth Dodson Gray, "Patriarchy as a Conceptual Trap" (Wellesley, Mass.: Roundtable Press, 1982), 17. Quoted in *Power and Authority: Issues for Women Clergy as Leaders* by Jeannette Sherrill (Middlesex, N.Y.: Hartford Seminary doctoral dissertation, 1990), 63.
5. Joel A. Barker, *The Business of Paradigms*, audiotape.
6. Ibid.
7. Loren B. Meade, *The Once and Future Church* (Washington, D.C.: The Alban Institute, 1991).
8. The dominant system in our culture is defined as white male because it is defined by those in power—specifically white men. Though men of other races sometimes benefit, they are at other times themselves outsiders. In religious circles, the white male system is often referred to as the patriarchy. I will use these terms interchangeably.
9. Gray, *Patriarchy as a Conceptual Trap*, 80, 86, 102. Quoted in Sherrill, 63.
10. Anne Wilson Schaef, *Women's Reality: An Emerging Female System in a White Male Society* (San Francisco: Harper & Row, 1981), 2. This small book has been applauded by women everywhere, including women in the church. The United Methodist Church Commission on the Status and Role of Women called it an "electrifying book . . . crucial for understanding the current dynamics of women's struggles to participate fully in the church and society."
11. Donna Schaper, *Common Sense About Men and Women in the Ministry* (Washington, D.C.: The Alban Institute, 1990), 16.
12. Schaef, *Women's Reality*, 5.
13. I am indebted to the thinking of Cornel West in *Race Matters* (Boston: Beacon Press, 1993). See also Lynn Rhodes, *Co-Creating: A Feminist Vision of Ministry* (Louisville: Westminster/John Knox Press, 1987), 55.
14. Letty Russell, *Church in the Round* (Louisville: Westminster/John Knox Press, 1993), 35-44.
15. Deborah L. Sheppard, "Organizations, Power, and Sexuality: The Image and Self-Image of Women Managers," *The Sexuality of Organization*, ed. Jeff Hearn, Deborah L. Sheppard, Peta Tancred-Sheriff, and Gibson Burrell (London: Sage Publications, 1989), 141.
16. Schaef, *Women's Reality*, 142.
17. Ann Machisale-Musopole, "Toward a New Ecumenical Movement: A Malawian Perspective," *Women and Church: The Challenge of Ecumenical Solidarity in an Age of Alienation*, ed. Melaine A. May (New York: Friendship Press, 1991), 144.
18. Russell, *Church in the Round*, 39.

19. Sheppard, "Organizations, Power, and Sexuality: The Image and Self-Image of Women Managers," *The Sexuality of Organization*, 142.

20. Donna Schaper, *Common Sense About Men and Women in the Ministry*, 10. Italics mine.

21. Judy Rosener, "Ways Women Lead," *Harvard Business Review* (November/December 1990): 119-20. Russell also gives a similar summary of women's style in *Church in the Round*, 67-73. Many other writers observing the church document the characteristics of women's leadership style. See also Anne Marie Nuechterlein and Celia A. Hahn, *The Male-Female Church Staff* (Washington, D.C.: The Alban Institute, 1990), 6-7; Marian Coger, *Women in Parish Ministry: Stress and Support* (Washington, D.C.: The Alban Institute, 1985), 11; "Toward a Renewed Community of Women and Men," by Joan Brown Campbell, "Ecumenical Leadership: Power and Women's Voices," by Kathleen S. Hurty, and "A Vision for Ecumenical Mission: Challenge During the Decade," by Mary Motte, F.M.M., in *Women and Church: The Challenge of Ecumenical Solidarity in an Age of Alienation* (New York: Friendship Press, 1991), 85, 93, 111.

22. It was Jung who formulated much of our description of feminine reality. "The psychic urge to relate, to join, to be in the midst of, to get involved with concrete feelings, things, and people" is the feminine principle. It should be active in both men and women. Cited by Sr. Suzanne Zuercher, in "Feminine Spirituality and Leadership in Ministry," unpublished paper, page 2; from *The Feminine in Jungian Psychology and Christian Theology* by Ann Belford Ulanov (Evanston, Ill.: Northwestern University Press, 1971), 154.

23. Sally Helgesen, *The Feminine Advantage: Women's Ways of Leadership* (New York: Doubleday, 1990), 55.

24. Deborah Tannen, *You Just Don't Understand* (New York: Ballantine, 1991), 24-25. Ann Wilson Schaef concurs in *Women's Reality*, 134.

25. Schaef, *Women's Reality*, 128.

26. Alicia Johnson, "Women Managers: Old Stereotypes Die Hard," *Management Review* (December 1987): 39.

27. Lynn R. Offerman and Cheryl Beil, "Achievement Styles of Women Leaders and Their Peers," *Psychology of Women Quarterly* 16: 1992, 53.

28. Nuechterlein and Hahn, *The Male-Female Church Staff*, 25.

29. Russell, *Church in the Round*, 57. See also her article "Feminism and the Church: A Quest for New Styles of Ministry," *Ministerial Formation* (October 1991): 29-30.

30. Nuechterlein and Hahn, *The Male-Female Church Staff*, 3.

31. Jean Lipman-Blumen, "Connective Leadership: Female Leadership Styles in the 21st Century Workplace," *Sociological Perspectives* 35:1, 183-203.

32. See chapter 2.

33. Schaef, *Women's Reality*, 40-41.

34. Albert J. Mills, "Gender, Sexuality, and Organizational Theory," *The Sexuality of Organization*, 42; also in Offerman and Beil, 38.

35. Sheppard, "Organizations, Power, and Sexuality: The Image and Self-Image of Women Managers," *The Sexuality of Organization*, 141.

36. See especially Edward C. Lehman, Jr., *Gender and Work: The Case of the Clergy* (New York: State University of New York, 1993). Research on women clergy in a broader context is now being updated by Jackson, Hargrove, and Lummis

at Hartford Seminary. As part of the preliminary reporting of that research, Adair Lummis has written an article entitled "Feminist Values and Other Influences on Pastoral Leadership Styles: Does Gender Matter?" for the Society for the Scientific Study of Religion, November 1994. This work is funded by the Lilly Endowment.

37. Rosener, "Ways Women Lead," *Harvard Business Review* (November/December 1990): 125. Amy Saltzman corroborates this view in "Trouble at the Top," *U.S. News and World Report*, 17 June 1990, 44. See also Tannen, *You Just Don't Understand*, 17.

38. For a Darwinian analysis of the debate about differences, see "Feminists, Meet Mr. Darwin," by Robert Wright in *The New Republic*, 28 November 1994, 34-46. Lehman also provides an exhaustive summary of the various points of view in the debate about differences in *Gender and Work: The Case of the Clergy.* See also Anne Roiphe, "Talking Trouble," *Working Woman*, October 1994, 30.

39. Ann M. Morrison, *The New Leaders: Guidelines on Leadership Diversity in America* (San Francisco: Jossey-Bass Publishers, 1992), 34.

40. Barbara Presley Noble, "The Debate Over *la Différence*," *New York Times*, 15 August 1993. See also Sheppard, "Organizations, Power, and Sexuality," 141.

41. Patrick Z. McGavin, "Film She-Devils," The *Chicago Tribune*, 25 December 1994, Section 13, 16-17.

42. Schaef, *Women's Reality*, 41; Nuechterlein and Hahn, *The Male-Female Church Staff*, 32.

43. Carol Hymowitz and Timothy Schellhardt, "The Glass Ceiling, *Wall Street Journal Special Report*, 24 March 1986, 1.

44. Cathy Trost, "Women Managers Quit Not for Family but to Advance Their Corporate Climb," *Wall Street Journal*, Midwest Edition, 2 May 1990, B1. See also Hazel M. Rosin and Karen Korabik, "Workplace Variables, Affective Responses, and Intention to Leave Among Women Managers," *Journal of Occupational Psychology* 64:4 (December 1991): 317-30.

45. Felice N. Schwartz, "Management Women and the New Facts of Life," *Harvard Business Review* (January/February 1989): 68.

46. Leon E. Wynter, "Double Whammy Hinders 'Double Minorities,' " *Wall Street Journal*, 19 January 1994, B1. For this reason, Russell points to Alice Walker's well-known statement: "black women's experience is as different from white women's as purple is to lavender," *Church in the Round*, 27.

47. Johnson, "Women Managers: Old Stereotypes Die Hard," 37.

48. Martha Burk and Josh Feltman, "How to Get Paid More Really," *Executive Female* (January/February 1995): 46-7. See also Saltzman, "Trouble at the Top," *U.S. News and World Report*, 17 June 1990, 41; Rosener, "Ways Women Lead," *Harvard Business Review*, (November/December 1990): 121; Trost, "Women Managers Quit Not for Family but to Advance Their Corporate Climb," B1.

49. Patricia M. Y. Chang, "Women of the Cloth Part Two: Preliminary Findings of a Cross-Denominational Study of Men and Women Clergy from 16 Protestant Denominations," Hartford Seminary, 1994. Paper prepared for the 1994 Annual Meeting of the Association for the Sociology of Religion, 3-4. This paper is based on a study funded by the Lilly Endowment.

50. Constant H. Jacquet, "Women Ministers in 1986 and 1977: A Ten Year Review," Office of Research and Evaluation, National Council of Churches.

Cited by Mary D. Pellauer in *Twenty Years after the Ordination of Women* (Chicago: The Evangelical Lutheran Church in America, 1990), 1.

51. Edward C. Lehman, Jr., "Patterns of Lay Resistance to Women in Ministry," *Sociological Analysis* 41:4 (1981) and "Sexism, Organizational Maintenance, and Localism: A Research Note," *Sociological Analysis* 48:3 (1987). See also Lehman's newest study, *Gender and Work: The Case of Clergy*, 29. Lehman confirms findings of a 1983 study reported in *Women of the Cloth* by Jackson Carroll, Barbara Hargrove, and Adair T. Lummis (New York: Harper & Row, 1983), 5.

Carole Carlson, "Clergywomen and Senior Pastorates," *The Christian Century*, January 6-13, 1988, 15-17. These findings are verified more recently by Jeanette R. Sherrill, "Power and Authority: Issues for Women Clergy as Leaders," 2.

A study by Marjorie H. Royle does not show clearly that placement *problems* for women have been overcome. Her work was confined to women who have successfully found placement, and did not examine the length of time it took them to do so. Royle's study finds no placement *differences* in a study of four denominations with data tabulated together, but notes that when individual denominations in her study are tabulated separately, there are placement differences, with women going to smaller parishes or parishes with lower attendance. See "Women Pastors: What Happens After Placement?" *Review of Religious Research* 24:2 (December 1982): 120, 124.

52. Eileen W. Lindner, "Still In But Out," *Women and Church: The Challenge of Ecumenical Solidarity in an Age of Alienation* (New York: Friendship Press, 1991), 107.

53. The only research I did find is "Protestant Church Decision-Makers: A Profile," by William McKinney and David A. Olson, in *Yearbook of American and Canadian Churches* (New York: National Council of Churches of Christ, 1991). This research polled leadership in six Protestant denominations. Statistics show that about 32 percent overall are women.

54. Records may not be kept for men either. But men, who enjoy the opportunity to work in a familiar paradigm, do not need the same kind of attention to their success that women now need in the church. One would think that a denomination truly concerned about how women are doing in their roles as church leaders would undertake the research that would tell them.

55. Amalie Shannon, "A Lutheran Woman Looks at the Decades," *Women and Church: The Challenge of Ecumenical Solidarity in an Age of Alienation* (New York: Friendship Press, 1991), 60-64.

4. The Church as an Environment for Women

1. For a more thorough review of the relationship between religion and the feminine in psychology, see Patricia Martin Doyle, "Women and Religion: Psychological and Cultural Implications," *Religion and Sexism*, ed. Rosemary Radford Ruether (New York: Simon & Schuster, 1974), 9-32.

2. Jackson W. Carroll's recent call for reflective leadership among churchwomen and men is a case in point. Here is a man well known in Protestant circles who outlines a leadership style that is much more collaborative than it is hierarchical. It is the possibility of colleagues like this that gives women hope for their

acceptance in the church. *As One With Authority* (Louisville: Westminster/John Knox Press, 1991).

3. Anne Marie Nuechterlein and Celia A. Hahn, *The Male-Female Church Staff* (Washington, D.C.: The Alban Institute, 1990), 23.

4. Ibid., 24.

5. Ibid., 31.

6. Donna Schaper, *Common Sense About Men and Women in the Ministry* (Washington, D.C.: The Alban Institute, 1990), 69.

7. For a summary of the statistics on women in church leadership, see chapter 3.

8. Albert J. Mills, "Gender, Sexuality, and Organizational Theory," *The Sexuality of Organization*, ed. Jeff Hearn, Deborah L. Sheppard, Peta Tancred-Sheriff, and Gibson Burrell (London: Sage Publications, 1989), 39.

9. Letty Russell, *Church in the Round* (Louisville: Westminster/John Knox Press, 1993), 23. For many years, The Alban Institute has been documenting how this cognitive dissonance affects women, indicating, among other things, that women are seriously asking whether they can stay in the church. See "Does the Church Have Room for Women Like These?" by Celia Allison Hahn in *Action Information* 12:1 (January/February 1986): 4-6.

10. Ann Wilson Schaef, *Women's Reality: An Emerging Female System in a White Male Society* (San Francisco: Harper & Row, 1985), 164-67.

11. Ibid, 169.

12. Nuechterlein and Hahn, *The Male-Female Church Staff*, 10.

13. Carroll, *As One With Authority*, 63-76. Jean Bethke Elshtain adds an insightful comment on how Christianity retained the hierarchical order of the culture even as it created new paradigms of the individual's relationship to the state. See "Christianity and Patriarchy: The Odd Alliance," in *Modern Theology* 9:2 (April 1993): 114.

14. Christopher Bryan, "Feminism and Christianity," *Sewanee Theological Review* 35:4 (1992): 324.

15. Russell, *Church in the Round*, 12 and 47. She cites the work of Rosemary Radford Ruether, *WomenChurch: Theology and Practice of Feminist Liturgical Communities*, and Elisabeth Schüssler Fiorenza, *Bread Not Stone: The Challenge of Feminist Biblical Interpretation*, as most helpful in this regard.

16. Richard N. Ostling, "The Second Reformation," *Time*, 23 November 1992, 53-58. Much has happened since the publication of this overview. Anglican ordination is divisive of the Church of England and the Christian Reformed Church has voted, unvoted, and voted again to ordain women, among other developments.

17. Jackson W. Carroll, Barbara Hargrove, and Adair T. Lummis, *Women of the Cloth* (New York: Harper & Row, 1983), 47.

18. For an excellent summary of women's struggle to win the right to preach and the later struggles for ordination, see Barbara Brown Zikmund, "The Struggle for the Right to Preach" and "Winning Ordination for Women in Mainstream Protestant Churches," *Women and Religion in America* (New York: Harper & Row, 1983), 193-205 and 339-49.

19. The research by Carroll, et al., is being updated at the time of this writing. In the original findings, the authors point to institutional sexism as a major block for women in ministry. Even in denominations that do ordain women, sexism contributes to typecasting of women, the use of exclusively masculine language,

the marginality of the denominations, which causes latent sexism to rise to the surface, and the profession's role in guarding tradition, among which is the "sacredly masculine image of the clergy" (pages 206-10). Findings are largely supported by a study of attitudes toward ordination in the Church of England in 1987. See Nancy Nason-Clark, "Ordaining Women as Priests: Religious vs. Sexist Explanations for Clerical Attitudes," *Sociological Analysis* 48:3 (1987): 259-73.

20. Pamela W. Darling, *New Wine: The Story of Women Transforming Leadership and Power in the Episcopal Church* (Boston: Cowley Publications, 1994), 164.

21. Bryan, "Feminism and Christianity," in *Sewanee Theological Review* 35:4 (1992): 324.

22. Ursula Jane O'Shea, "Women in the Religious Society of Friends [Quakers]: The Relevance of Their Experience in Envisioning a Gender Inclusive Church," *Listening: Journal of Religion and Culture* 27:2 (Spring 1992): 145.

23. Donna Schaper, *Common Sense About Men and Women in the Ministry* (Washington, D.C.: The Alban Institute, 1990), 6-9.

24. Ann Carr, "Women, Justice and the Church," *Horizons* 17:2 (1990): 269-70.

25. Russell, *Church in the Round*, 68. She cites Jean Caffey Lyles, "Moves of the Spirit: Diversity or Syncretism?" *Christian Century*, 13 March 1991, 284-86.

26. Former Presbyterian staff liaison Mary Ann Lundy, quoted in denominational news releases.

27. For two different views of this event, see Katherine Kersten, "How the Feminist Establishment Hurts Women," *Christianity Today*, 20 June 1994, 24; and Janice Love, "Finding Space to Reimage God," *Sojourners*, May 1994, 8-9.

28. Letty Russell reminds us that in so doing, women follow the example of their foremother, Miriam. *Church in the Round*, 68.

29. Kathy is a pseudonym, and the details of this anecdote have been changed for the obvious need to protect the woman in question. The story is true.

30. Russell, *Church in the Round*, 160.

31. Rena M. Yocum, "Presents and Presence," *Women and Church: The Challenge of Ecumenical Solidarity in an Age of Alienation*, ed. Melanie May (New York: Friendship Press, 1991), 70-76.

32. Russell, *Church in the Round*, 160. She quotes Elisabeth Schüssler Fiorenza, *In Memory of Her*, 29; Schüssler Fiorenza, *Bread Not Stone*, xiv; and Russell, *Household of Freedom*, 29-42.

33. Nuechterlein and Hahn, in *The Male-Female Church Staff* (Washington, D.C.: The Alban Institute, 1990), 24, are much more optimistic on this point than I am.

34. Here I disagree with those who claim that authority presumes hierarchy. See, for example, J. I. Packer, "Understanding the Differences," in *Women, Authority, and the Bible* (Downers Grove, Ill.: Intervarsity Press, 1986), 291.

35. Russell, *Church in the Round*, 170.

36. I use here Margaret Bendroth's definition of fundamentalism and its neoevangelical offspring: those denominations which are "culturally and theologically conservative" and include denominations as diverse as the Southern Baptists, the Missouri Synod Lutherans, the Christian Reformed Church, the Assemblies of God, The Evangelical Free Church, and others. See *Fundamentalism and Gender: 1875 to the Present* (New Haven, Conn.: Yale University Press, 1993), 4-5. There are also many predominantly black denominations which

have conservative views of the leadership of women. Some may be considered a part of the neoevangelical tradition. Others are in the Pentecostal tradition. These include the African Methodist Episcopal, the Church of God in Christ and others. See Helen T. Gray, "Women's Leadership Roles Challenge Tradition," *Progressions* (February 1992): 14-16.

37. For comments on the theology that undergirds this silencing, see chapter 6.

38. Margaret Bendroth, "Fundamentalism and Femininity: The Reorientation of Women's Role in the 1920s," *Evangelical Studies Bulletin* 5:1 (March 1988): 1-2. See also Bendroth, *Fundamentalism and Gender: 1875 to the Present*, 1-12.

39. Janette Hassey, *No Time for Silence: Evangelical Women in Public Ministry Around the Turn of the Century* (Grand Rapids: Zondervan, 1986), 137, and Michael Hamilton, "Women, Public Ministry, and American Fundamentalism, 1920–1950," *Religion and American Culture* 3:2 (Summer 1993): 171-96, and Edith Blumhofer, "Women in Evangelicalism and Pentecostalism," *Women and Church: The Challenge of Ecumenical Solidarity in an Age of Alienation*, ed. Melanie May (New York: Friendship Press, 1991), 3-7.

40. A review of the literature of fundamentalism points out two overriding concerns of its writers: reconstructing the history of women in leadership, often from original sources, since often official records of the work of women do not exist; and continuing the seemingly endless theological debate about women in leadership. I address this second trend in chapter 5.

41. Margaret Bendroth, "Fundamentalism and Femininity: The Reorientation of Women's Role in the 1920s," 2.

42. Hamilton, "Women, Public Ministry, and American Fundamentalism, 1920–1950," 171-96.

43. Blumhofer points out that although Pentecostal churches are often thought of as more open to the leadership of women, it is not necessarily so. Women there fare little better than their sisters in neoevangelicalism. "Women in Evangelicalism and Pentecostalism," 6.

44. Patricia M. Y. Chang, "Women of the Cloth Part Two: Preliminary Findings of a Cross Denominational Study of Men and Women Clergy from 16 Protestant Denominations," Hartford Seminary, 1994, paper prepared for the 1994 Annual Meeting of the Association for the Sociology of Religion, 4. This study is funded by the Lilly Endowment.

45. Sarah Frances Anders and Marilyn Metcalf-Whittaker, "Women as Lay Leaders and Clergy: A Critical Issue," in *Southern Baptists Observed*, ed. Nancy Tatom Ammerman (Knoxville: University of Tennessee Press, 1993), 219.

46. Ruth A. Wallace, "Bringing Women In: Marginality in the Churches," *Sociological Analysis* 36:4 (1975): 293.

47. Associated Baptist Press releases 18 August 1994.

48. Letty Russell, "Searching for a Round Table in Church and World," *Women and Church: The Challenge of Ecumenical Solidarity in an Age of Alienation*, 173.

49. For two fine personal accounts which answer this question, see Diana Hochstedt Butler, "Between Two Worlds," *The Christian Century* 3 March 1993: 231-2 and Stefanie Yova Yazge, "From One Orthodox Woman's Perspective," *Women and Church: The Challenge of Ecumenical Solidarity in an Age of Alienation*, 65-69.

50. Rita Nakashima Brock, "On Remembering What Is Impossible to Forget," *Women and Church: The Challenge of Ecumenical Solidarity in an Age of Alienation*, 11.

5. The Sexuality of Denominations

1. Celia Allison Hahn, "A Conversation with Henry Berne," *Action Information* 5:3 (May/June 1979): 8.
2. I am indebted here to the thinking of British sociologists Jeff Hearn and Gibson Burrell. See "The Sexuality of Organization," *The Sexuality of Organization*, ed. Jeff Hearn, Deborah L. Sheppard, Peta Tancred-Sheriff, and Gibson Burrell (London: Sage Publications, 1989), 1-28.
3. Rosemary Radford Ruether, *New Woman, New Earth: Sexist Ideologies and Human Liberation* (New York: Crossroads Books, 1975), 3.
4. Hearn and Burrell, *The Sexuality of Organization*, 5. See also Lynn Rhodes, *Co-Creating: A Feminist Vision for Ministry* (Louisville: Westminster/John Knox Press, 1987), 62.
5. Hearn and Burrell, *The Sexuality of Organization*, 13, 15.
6. Ibid., 10.
7. This idea was first articulated by Simone de Beauvior in *The Second Sex*.
8. See Beverly Wildung Harrison, "Human Sexuality and Mutuality," *Christian Feminism: Visions for a New Humanity*, ed. Judith Weidman (New York: Harper & Row, 1984), 141-46, and Jean Bethke Elsthain, "Christianity and Patriarchy: The Odd Alliance," *Modern Theology* 9:2 (April 1993): 109-22.
9. Janette Hassey, "Brief History of Christian Feminism," *Transformation* 6:2 (April/June 1989): 2.
10. George H. Tavard, *Woman in Christian Tradition* (Notre Dame: University of Notre Dame Press, 1973), 125. This is a view we can still find prevalent in many Protestant denominations today.
11. Bernard Prusak gives a fine summary of canonical, apocryphal, and pseudoepigraphal literature in which woman is held accountable for the Fall. See "Woman: Seductive Siren and Source of Sin?" *Religion and Sexism*, ed. Rosemary Radford Ruether (New York: Simon & Schuster, 1974), 89-107. The Jewish patriarchy also adopted these thought streams as early as 1000 BCE, with the adaptation of the male monarchy in Israel.
12. Rosemary Radford Ruether, "Misogynism and Virginal Feminism in the Fathers of the Church," *Religion and Sexism*, 161-3: "Augustine believes that the seat of this disordered affection due to sin is the male penis, whose spontaneous tumescence, in response to sensual stimuli and independent of consciousness, is the literal embodiment of that 'law in the members that wars against the law of the minds.' (She cites the *Confessions* as follows: *De Civitate Dei*, 14, 24; *De Grat. Chr. et de Pecc. Orig.*, 2, 41; *De Nupt. et Concup.* I, 6-7, 21, 33) . . . But if the male erection was the essence of sin, woman, as its source, became peculiarly the cause, object and extension of it. This, as we have noted, results in an essentially depersonalized view of the relationship to woman."
13. For a thorough treatment of this subject, see *Veiled and Silenced: How Culture Shaped Sexist Theology* by Alvin John Schmidt (Macon, Ga.: Mercer University Press, 1989).

14. Elaine Pagels, *Adam, Eve, and the Serpent* (New York: Random House, 1988), xvii.

15. Ann Wilson Schaef concurs in *Women's Reality: An Emerging Female System in a White Male Society* (San Francisco: Harper & Row, 1985), 114.

16. Ruether, "Misogynism and Virginal Feminism in the Fathers of the Church," in *Religion and Sexism*, 163.

17. For an excellent essay on the ways in which fundamentalism seeks to control the power of women, see Karen McCarthy Brown, "Fundamentalism and the Control of Women," *Fundamentalism and Gender*, ed. John Stratton Hawley (New York: Oxford University Press, 1994), 175-201. "Stress from almost any source, if sufficiently strong, will provoke a need to control the dangerous power of women. The crucial psychological fact is that all of us, male and female, fear the will of woman." She continues, citing Dorothy Dinnerstein: "fear of the female will, when combined with deep memories of the joy and security found in the woman's presence, produce a powerful ambivalence toward women that is apparent in the myths, religious practices, social structures, and daily interactions of people around the world. In one moment woman is a goddess, the next she is a voracious, polluting monster."

18. Gertrude Jobes, *Dictionary of Mythology, Folklore and Symbols* (New York: Scarecrow Press, 1962).

19. Carol E. Becker, "In Any Age: Can We Hear God?" *New Age Spirituality: An Assessment*, ed. Duncan S. Ferguson (Louisville: Westminster/John Knox Press, 1989), 24.

20. Irene Claremont de Castillejo, *Knowing Woman: A Feminine Psychology* (San Francisco: Harper & Row, 1974), 77-78.

21. Paul G. Bretscher, in "Culture Virus," *Lutheran Forum* 26:3 (August 1992): 18, distinguishes between the biblical wisdom, which "perceives a factor inherent in maleness from God himself . . . by which man can fulfill God-ordained headship toward women." He adds: "The culture virus, [which] by contrast perceives maleness as itself the cause of women's sense of inferiority." He asserts that "these wisdoms are incompatible." Arguments like this make sense when viewed from within the white male system. Outside that paradigm, they do not make sense.

22. Prusak, "Woman: Seductive Siren and Source of Sin?" *Religion and Sexism*, 107. The author believes that men have overcome this need. I would not agree. There is still too much evidence to the contrary.

23. Arguments by a conservative denomination, which would remove women from teaching on Sunday and even singing in church choirs make no sense when viewed outside this perspective. When understood inside this perspective they not only "make sense" but are taken seriously. This example is only one of many that can be found in the literature.

24. Schaef, *Women's Reality*, 164. Anyone who denies that this idolatry is alive in the church should observe the reaction within one denomination, whose magazine cover depicted a black Christ on the cross for a recent Easter edition. It proved to be the cover that generated more protest than any cover in the history of the magazine.

25. For a fine article that gives life to the work of a variety of feminist theologians, see Cullen Murphy, "Women and the Bible," *The Atlantic Monthly*, August 1993, 39-64.

26. Rosemary Radford Ruether, "Feminist Theology and Spirituality," *Christian Feminism*, 10.

27. I am indebted to Ruether's overview of feminist theology for this short summary, *Christian Feminism*, 10-12. See also Elisabeth Schüssler Fiorenza, *In Memory of Her* (New York: Crossroads, 1989); Elizabeth Johnson, *She Who Is: The Mystery of God in Feminist Theological Discourse* (New York: Crossroads, 1992).

28. Elisabeth Schüssler Fiorenza, "Emerging Issues in Feminist Biblical Interpretation," *Christian Feminism*, 34.

29. Letty Russell, "Two Become One," *Sewanee Theological Review* 35:4 (1992), 339.

30. Johnson, *She Who Is: The Mystery of God in Feminist Theological Discourse*, 61.

31. Margaret O'Gara, "Ecumenism and Feminism in Dialogue on Authority," *Women and Church: The Challenge of Ecumenical Solidarity in an Age of Alienation*, ed. Melanie A. May (New York: Friendship Press, 1991), 130.

32. Letty Russell, "Women and Ministry: Problem or Possibility?" *Christian Feminism*, 78.

33. Elisabeth Schüssler Fiorenza, "Emerging Issues in Feminist Biblical Interpretation," *Christian Feminism*, 35.

34. They are criticized for not allowing for universal principles. Letty Russell gives a thorough analysis of this criticism, rejecting it in the end. See *Church in the Round* (Louisville: Westminster/John Knox Press, 1993), 32-33. Margaret O'Gara points out that feminist theologies can too quickly project evil onto others: men, the church, and patriarchy, forgetting that women too are implicit in sin. See "Ecumenism and Feminism in Dialogue on Authority," *Women and Church, The Challenge of Ecumenical Solidarity in an Age of Alienation*, 132.

35. Pagels, *Adam, Eve, and the Serpent*, xxiii.

36. Lora Gross and Ted Peters, "Role Models for Women Seminarians," *Dialog* 28:2 (Spring 1989): 95.

37. Johnson, *She Who Is*; Virginia Ramey Mollenkott, *Sensuous Spirituality* (New York: Crossroads, 1993). Many other feminist theologians deal extensively with the issue of language.

38. Women and men both need feminine names for God. Elizabeth Johnson explains why in a most compelling argument. She also shows that we are unable to see the whole of God in the feminine.

39. Ted Peters, "Worship Wars," *Dialog* 33:3 (Summer 1994): 171-72 italics mine. Peters does not necessarily espouse this dichotomy, but uses it to explain differences between what he calls the "biblical symbol camp" and the "God-inclusive forces."

40. *The Jerusalem Bible* (New York: Doubleday, 1971), 223.

41. Cullen Murphy, "Women and the Bible," 48.

42. Rena Yocum, "Presents and Presence," *Women and Church*, 72.

43. Paul Jewett, *The Ordination of Women* (Grand Rapids: Eerdmans, 1980), 129, quoting Martin Luther King, Jr., *Where Do We Go From Here?* (New York: Harper & Row, 1967), 41.

44. Jewett, *The Ordination of Women*, 141, quoting *Children's Letters to God*, ed. Eric Marshall and Stuart Hample (London: Collins, 1967).

Part Two—Organizational Wives or New Paradigm Leaders?

1. Ann S. Huff, "Wives of the Organization," 3. Originally presented at the Women and Work Conference, Arlington, Texas, May 11, 1990.
2. Rosener and Helgesen, both cited in the first chapter, are among those making the claim that "things will be better" for women because of their relational skills. John Naisbitt agrees.
3. Arlie Russell Hochschild, *The Managed Heart: Commercialization of Human Feeling* (Berkeley: University of California Press, 1983), 170.
4. Ibid., 7. See also Albert J. Mills, "Gender, Sexuality and Organizational Theory," *The Sexuality of Organization*, ed. Jeff Hearn, Deborah L. Sheppard, Peta Tancred-Sheriff, and Gibson Burrell (London: Sage Publications, 1989), 34-5.
5. Anne Marie Nuechterlein and Celia A. Hahn, *The Male-Female Church Staff* (Washington, D.C.: The Alban Institute, 1990), 30. They credit K. R. Mitchell, in *Multiple Staff Ministries* (Philadelphia: Westminster, 1988) for this example.
6. The stories of both these women are told in the opening section of chapter 2.
7. Letty Russell, *Church in the Round* (Louisville: Westminster/John Knox Press, 1993), 51-52.
8. Nuechterlein and Hahn, *The Male-Female Church Staff*, 24.
9. Donna Schaper, *Common Sense About Men and Women in the Ministry* (Washington, D.C.: The Alban Institute, 1990), 122.
10. Marian Coger, *Women in Parish Ministry: Stress and Support* (Washington, D.C.: The Alban Institute, 1991), 4-5, citing Rosabeth Moss Kanter, *Men and Women of the Corporation* (New York: Basic Books, 1977), 209.
11. All of the experiences recounted in this section are based on incidents in the lives of women and men who work for mainline denominations. Names have been changed to protect the identity of those reporting.

6. The Incredible, Invisible Woman

1. Marian Coger, *Women in Parish Ministry: Stress and Support* (Washington, D.C.: The Alban Institute, 1991), 16, quoting Margaret E. Howe, *Women and Church Leadership* (Grand Rapids: Zondervan, 1982), 195.
2. Ibid., 16. She uses this example in reference to clergywomen. I extend it to other women in leadership as well.
3. Ibid., 16, quoting M. Helene Pollock, "Growing Toward Effective Ministry," *Women Ministers*, ed. Judith L. Weidman (San Francisco: Harper & Row, 1981), 16.
4. Ibid., 16.
5. Deborah L. Sheppard, "Organizations, Power, and Sexuality: The Image and Self-Image of Women Managers," *The Sexuality of Organization*, ed. Jeff Hearn, Deborah L. Sheppard, Peta Tancred-Sheriff, and Gibson Burrell (London: Sage Publications, 1989), 145.
6. Coger, *Women in Parish Ministry: Stress and Support*, 16.
7. Nancy Sehested, "A Southern Baptist Pastor Speaks," *Women and Church: The Challenge of Ecumenical Solidarity in an Age of Alienation*, ed. Melanie A. May (New York: Friendship Press, 1991), 57.

8. Coger, *Women in Parish Ministry: Stress and Support*, 16, cites studies by Lehman (1977) and Carroll, Hargrove, and Lummis (1981).
9. Ibid., 16, quoting Howe, *Women and Church Leadership*, 195.
10. Sehested, "A Southern Baptist Pastor Speaks," *Women and Church: The Challenge of Ecumenical Solidarity in an Age of Alienation*, 57.
11. Anne Marie Nuechterlein, and Celia A. Hahn, *The Male-Female Church Staff* (Washington, D.C.: The Alban Institute, 1990), 42.
12. Ibid., 42. Clergymen as well as clergywomen may struggle with voicelessness, because they do not often fit the stereotype of the strong, expert male, and because the church as an institution has lost the authority that was once unquestioned.
13. Ibid., 42, citing Belenky, et al., *Women's Ways of Knowing* (New York: Basic Books, 1986).
14. Deborah Tannen, *You Just Don't Understand* (New York: Ballantine Books, 1990), 133. The specific ways in which this phenomenon and others play out in the workplace are discussed in her more recent book, *Talking from 9 to 5* (New York: Morrow, 1994).
15. Ibid., 215.
16. Ibid., 228.
17. Coger, *Women in Parish Ministry; Stress and Support*, 10.
18. Ibid., 17.
19. Ibid., 17, citing Rosabeth Moss Kanter, *Men and Women of the Corporation* (New York: Basic Books, 1977), 166-69, 172, 189, 192, 197-200.
20. Ibid., 18.
21. Belle Rose Ragins and Eric Sundstrom, "Gender and Power in Organization: A Longitudinal Perspective," *Psychological Bulletin* 105:1 (1989): 59.
22. All three of these examples came to light as a result of interviews with original sources.

7. The Cinderella Syndrome

1. Said *USA Today* in a recent report: "Even Reno's ideological adversaries acknowledge a visible improvement in Justice's day-to-day operation. But management improvements are more a reflection of the prowess of [Deputy Attorney General Jamie] Gorelick than of Reno . . . Gorelick . . . is a 'deputy that has the ability to get things done, make decisions, keep things moving.' Critics still complain that Reno's experience as a county prosecutor hardly prepared her for the complexities of the attorney general's job." See "Reno's Pull Helped Push Crime Bill," by Sam Vincent Meddis and Bill Nichols, *USA Today*, 14 September 1994.
2. For a fuller discussion of language issues, see chapter 5.
3. *The Sexuality of Organization*, ed. Jeff Hearn, Deborah L. Sheppard, Peta Tancred-Sheriff, and Gibson Burrell (London: Sage Publications, 1989).
4. Sheppard, "Organizations, Power, and Sexuality: The Image and Self-Image of Women Managers," *The Sexuality of Organization*, 145.
5. Associated Baptist Press releases August 23, 1994.
6. Women in this study acted likewise. Most women interviewed were uncomfortable with the idea that they might be identifiable or that the information they shared might be used explicitly. They genuinely didn't want to act like

victims, but they also feared retaliation. Almost all emphasized that they were speaking "not to be complaining," but because they genuinely wanted the issues to be clarified.

7. Nancy Sehested, "A Southern Baptist Pastor Speaks," *Women and Church: The Challenge of Ecumenical Solidarity in an Age of Alienation*, ed. Melanie A. May (New York: Friendship Press, 1991), 57.

8. Albert J. Mills, "Gender, Sexuality and Organizational Theory," *The Sexuality of Organization*, ed. Jeff Hearn, Deborah L. Sheppard, Peta Tancred-Sheriff, and Gibson Burrell (London: Sage Publications, 1989), 38.

9. Ibid.

10. Ibid.

11. Susan Faludi, *Backlash: The Undeclared War Against American Women* (New York: Crown Publishers, 1991).

12. Mills, "Gender, Sexuality and Organizational Theory," *The Sexuality of Organization*, 36.

13. Ibid., 38.

14. Ibid., 39.

15. Marian Coger, *Women in Parish Ministry: Stress and Support* (Washington, D.C.: The Alban Institute, 1991), 23.

16. Ibid., 20-21.

17. Ibid., 21.

18. Faludi, *Backlash: The Undeclared War Against American Women*, chapter 3.

19. Coger, *Women in Parish Ministry; Stress and Support*, 43. She cites Rosabeth Moss Kanter, *Men and Women of the Corporation* (New York: Basic Books, 1977), 209.

20. Alison Bass, "Talking to Men, a Bold Woman Just Can't Win," *Boston Globe*, 7 January 1991, Section 3, 33.

8. Harassment and Other Hazards

1. Barbara A. Gutek, "Sexuality in the Workplace: Key Issues in Social Research and Organizational Practice," *The Sexuality of Organization*, ed. Jeff Hearn, Deborah L. Sheppard, Peta Tancred-Sheriff, and Gibson Burrell (London: Sage Publications, 1989), 58.

2. Nancy DiTomaso, "Sexuality in the Workplace: Discrimination and Harassment," *The Sexuality of Organization*, 72-3.

3. Gutek, "Sexuality in the Workplace: Key Issues in Social Research and Organizational Practice," *The Sexuality of Organization*, 68.

4. Ibid., 70.

5. Kenneth W. Inskeep and Jacqueline Mroczek, "Sexual Harassment Study Report," Evangelical Lutheran Church in America, January 25, 1993.

6. A quite different example from a clergywoman serves to illustrate comments about a woman's body that are not harassment. She says: "The number one comment I get more than anything else is shock that I am so short. People are stunned. I'll get twenty people easy, every time I preach. People say, 'I never thought you would be this short.' " Though invasive in their way of spotlighting the woman's body type, these comments do not seem to me to represent harassment because they are not in any way ridiculing.

7. Gutek, "Sexuality in the Workplace: Key Issues in Social Research and Organizational Practice," *The Sexuality of Organization*, 64. See also Deborah L. Sheppard, "Organizations, Power, and Sexuality: The Image and Self-Image of Women Managers," *The Sexuality of Organization*, 153-4.

8. Letty Russell, *Church in the Round* (Louisville: Westminster/John Knox Press, 1993), 52.

9. Gutek, "Sexuality in the Workplace: Key Issues in Social Research and Organizational Practice," *The Sexuality of Organization*, 65.

10. Ann Wilson Schaef, *Women's Reality: An Emerging Female System in a White Male Society* (San Francisco: Harper & Row, 1985), 114.

11. Gutek, "Sexuality in the Workplace: Key Issues in Social Research and Organizational Practice," *The Sexuality of Organization*, 59.

12. Ibid.

13. Russell, *Church in the Round*, 188.

14. Gutek, "Sexuality in the Workplace: Key Issues in Social Research and Organizational Practice," *The Sexuality of Organization*, 59-61.

15. This is true for both women and men. Letty Russell reminds us that "our sexuality as male and female is the embodiment of our spirituality," *Church in the Round*, 189.

16. Gutek, "Sexuality in the Workplace: Key Issues in Social Research and Organizational Practice," *The Sexuality of Organization*, 61.

17. Ibid., 62.

18. There is some evidence from men that looks may be more of a factor for them as well these days. Says one man: "Unless he starts his own company and surrounds himself with ugly workers, 'looks' for men are also crucial to advancement into the top ranks. Most women do not know what it feels like to present a brilliant plan for a new database and have to grin about a joke from a vice-president about that short bald guy who writes long memos. Yes, it's the male domination system, but only the fittest males break the glass ceiling too." This man also cites recent data on senators and presidents which reveals something we probably know but might not have thought about: only a handful in this century have been shorter than 5' 10"; most are over 6'. He concludes: "Only the pretty can win in the information age." This seems a legitimate response, though I have two cautions: First, women may not know what it's like to be chided for baldness, but they do know what it's like to be ridiculed for their looks. Second, women are more subject than are men to ridicule with sexual overtones. See chapter 8 for more on men and harassment.

19. Marian Coger, *Women in Parish Ministry: Stress and Support* (Washington, D.C.: The Alban Institute, 1991), 33.

20. Judy Rosener, "Ways Women Lead," *Harvard Business Review* (November/December 1990): 122-4.

21. Russell, *Church in the Round*, 186.

22. Coger, *Women in Parish Ministry: Stress and Support*, 35.

23. Nancy Sehested, "A Southern Baptist Pastor Speaks," *Women and Church: The Challenge of Ecumenical Solidarity in an Age of Alienation*, ed. Melanie A. May (New York: Friendship Press, 1991), 58.

24. Coger, *Women in Parish Ministry: Stress and Support*, 33.

9. Traps for Men

1. This is true even in the church, where there still exist many situations in which a hierarchical or authoritarian style may be expected by the organization, but a collaborative style is more natural for the leader, especially the female leader. See *The Male-Female Church Staff* by Anne Marie Nuechterlein and Celia A. Hahn (Washington, D.C.: The Alban Institute, 1990), 22-3; Marian Coger, *Women in Parish Ministry: Stress and Support* (Washington, D.C.: The Alban Institute, 1985), 11; and Kathleen S. Hurty, "Ecumenical Leadership: Power and Women's Voices," *Women and Church: The Challenge of Ecumenical Solidarity in an Age of Alienation*, ed. Melanie A. May (New York: Friendship Press, 1991), 93.
2. Obviously, some of the traps women encounter, especially those relating to their appearance and physical safety, are not experienced by men in the same way unless the men are homosexual or suspected to be homosexual.
3. Without getting into an argument about whether this is a male trait, we can safely say that men do learn how to take charge. They are schooled by their upbringing, by the influence of organized sports, and by the competitive environment of the workplace, where they remain at the center of activity and power. Women, of course, must also learn to be competitive to succeed. We all work in a culture that is based on competition and rewards winners. How women might be outside this paradigm is impossible to know.
4. Barbara Gutek, "Sexuality in the Workplace: Key Issues in Social Research and Organizational Practice," *The Sexuality of Organization*, ed. Jeff Hearn, Deborah L. Sheppard, Peta Tancred-Sheriff, and Gibson Burrell (London: Sage Publications, 1989), 56-7.
5. Ibid., 59.
6. I have mentioned this trap in passing in chapter 5 and chapter 8. Here I want to address it more completely.
7. Gutek, "Sexuality in the Workplace: Key Issues in Social Research and Organizational Practice," *The Sexuality of Organization*, 60.
8. This is a common trap for husbands and wives.

Part Three—Changing and Growing Together

1. On this one point I would disagree. Men are "bumping up against women's ways of doing things" as they learn to take an active role in the family and household.
2. Donna Schaper, *Common Sense About Men and Women in the Ministry* (Washington, D.C.: The Alban Institute, 1990), 14.
3. Ann Wilson Schaef described a number of different "helpful" stances men take toward women in *Women's Reality: An Emerging Female System in a White Male Society* (San Francisco: Harper & Row, 1985), 64-5. For a fuller discussion of men and their response to women's concerns, see chapter 10.

10. What Men Must Do

1. Anne Wilson Schaef, *Women's Reality: An Emerging Female System in a White Male Society* (San Francisco: Harper & Row, 1985), 8-10.

2. Ibid., 64-66.
3. Marianne Coger, *Women in Parish Ministry: Stress and Support* (Washington, D.C.: The Alban Institute, 1991), 24.
4. Anne Wilson Schaef's comments parallel mine in many ways, particularly her recognition of the men who listen. See 64-6.
5. George Tunick, "Re-Educating Chauvinists," *Executive Female* (January/February 1995): 82.
6. " 'Does the Church Have Room for Women Like These?' A Response from Edward W. Bauman," *Action Information* 12:2, 6.
7. The workshop is offered by Men Stopping Violence, Atlanta, Georgia. Judging from the feedback I received from men in several denominations, it is a powerful and life-changing experience. Rita Nakashima Brock writes of another similar experience for both sexes, offered by the National Conference of Christians and Jews. It is called the Brotherhood/Sisterhood Camp. See "The Feminist Redemption of Christ," *Christian Feminism*, ed. Judith Weidman (San Francisco: Harper & Row, 1984), 55-56.
8. "Men Working with Women Against Violence: 'Liberating Potential' for the Mennonite Church," in *Gospel Herald*, 15 February 1994, 8. This article is a collection of riveting comments by both men and women who have participated in the event.
9. Bruce Burnham, "Men Stopping Violence," *Common Lot* (Spring 1994): 12.
10. Donna Schaper, *Common Sense About Men and Women in the Ministry* (Washington, D.C.: The Alban Institute, 1990), 13.
11. John Wesley had a similar experience, which is retold in Paul W. Chilcote, *She Offered Them Christ* (Nashville: Abingdon Press, 1993), 20. His mother Susanna led public worship for her clergyman husband while he was attending Parliament during the winters of 1710–12. To the chagrin of the cleric that Wesley left in charge, Susanna's services attracted hundreds. "Susanna handed down a legacy of faith to her son in which one's conviction remained primary. No one, not even a woman, ought to be prohibited from doing God's work in obedience to the inner calling of her conscience. Wesley never forgot."
12. Some men who have neither the mother influence nor the life-changing moment miss the opportunity. They are literally never as able to accept women as full partners. When asked the question, "What has prepared you to work with women?" They seem mystified by the question. It is as though they are unaware that they need any preparation.
13. Carolyn Ferguson Hunt, "How to Meet the Needs of Women on Your Team," *Evangelical Missions Quarterly* (April 1990): 179.

11. The Mathematics of Power

1. Not her real name.
2. Jeannette Sherrill, "Power and Authority: Issues for Women Clergy as Leaders" (Middlesex, N.Y.: Hartford Seminary doctoral dissertation, 1990), 44. She cites Jean Baker Miller, *Toward a New Psychology of Women* (Boston: Beacon Press, 1986), 83.
3. Rosemary Chinnici, *Can Women Re-Image the Church?* (New York: Paulist Press, 1992), 34. She cites Michael Lerner, *Surplus Powerlessness* (Oakland: Institute for

Labor and Mental Health, 1986). The commitment to failure is strong enough in women that they often *redefine their success as failure.*

4. In asking this question, we would be wise to remember that ordination is conferred by a small, bureaucratic group of church leaders in a hierarchical system that masks many defining issues, including doctrine, pedigree, benefactors, demographics, and fiscal constraints as well as gender.

5. Anita Anand, "Of Virtue and Power," *Christian Social Action* (October 1990): 25.

6. Donna Schaper, *Common Sense About Men and Women in the Ministry* (Washington, D.C.: The Alban Institute, 1990), 6.

7. Martha Ellen Stortz, *Pastor Power* (Nashville: Abingdon Press, 1993), 8.

8. Sherrill, *Power and Authority: Issues for Women Clergy as Leaders,* 44, citing Jean Baker Miller, "Women and Power," *Work in Progress* (Wellesley, Mass.: Stone Center, 1982), 2; also Schaper, *Common Sense About Men and Women in the Ministry,* 86.

9. I am much in debt to Martha Stortz for the foregoing delineation of power and for this point. See *Pastor Power,* 18. See also her theological discussion of the legitimacy of each of the forms of power, *Pastor Power,* 129.

10. Schaper, *Common Sense About Men and Women in the Ministry,* 77.

11. Ibid., 81.

12. See Lynn Rhodes, *Co-Creating: A Feminist Vision of Ministry* (Philadelphia: Westminster Press, 1987), 29.

13. Stortz summarizes a number of typical biases about power held by women and other ethnic minority groups as a result of this misunderstanding. The most radical: "As a matter of principle, many minority groups tacitly agree neither to exercise nor to analyze power." She includes women. See *Pastor Power,* 51-2.

14. Ibid., 109.

15. Ibid., 32-3 and 36-7. See also Jackson Carroll, *As One with Authority* (Louisville: Westminster/John Knox Press, 1991), 37. Current discussion on this subject is much indebted to the work of Hannah Arendt in *The Human Condition* (Chicago: University of Chicago Press, 1958).

16. Carol Noren, *The Woman in the Pulpit* (Nashville: Abingdon Press, 1991), 47, 49-51. She points out many specific reasons a woman may feel this greater comfort in exercising power, among them the fact that in the pulpit, she will not be shouted down.

17. Schaper, *Common Sense About Men and Women in the Ministry,* 59.

18. "Going public" requires three powers of the leader: the power to define, the power to name, and the power to delineate space. See Stortz, *Pastor Power,* 20.

19. Schaper, *Common Sense About Men and Women in the Ministry,* 108.

20. Ibid., 110.

21. Ibid., 107-9.

22. Ibid., 13.

23. Ibid., 62.

24. Lora Gross and Ted Peters, "Role Models for Women Seminarians," *Dialog* 28:2 (Spring 1989): 99. Gross and Peters address a specific aspect of mentoring in identifying the importance of female role models for female seminary students. The primary need, they say, is for women to have empowering rather than pedagogical role models.

25. Women talked about the need to be themselves in chapter 2. In chapter 8, we summarized the "Be Yourself" traps.
26. Ann S. Huff, "Wives of the Organization," 16-21. Originally presented at the Women and Work Conference, Arlington, Texas, May 11, 1990.
27. Stortz, *Pastor Power,* 67-8 and 122.
28. Marian Coger, *Women in Parish Ministry: Stress and Support* (Washington, D.C.: The Alban Institute, 1985), 19.
29. Schaper, *Common Sense About Men and Women in the Ministry,* 74.
30. Ibid., 71, 73.